THE HISTORY OF
THE CULTURE OF WAR

by David Adams

2008

© David Adams, 2008

Second printing, July 2009 (with corrections)

Contact: david@cpnn-world.org

ISBN 1441480986
EAN-13: 9781441480989

Available for reading on-line or for mail-order at
http://culture-of-peace.info/books/history.html

Cover photos were taken by the author.
They show the courtyard of Ecole Militaire
in Paris where Napoleon was trained.
Illustrated are helicopters, horsemanship,
marching band, volleyball and a formal
ceremony with men in uniform.
(See p. 149 for explanation.)

TABLE OF CONTENTS

What is culture and how does it evolve? ……...….……1

Warfare in prehistory and its usefulness ………....……..3

The culture of war in prehistory …….……………...……..16

Data from prehistory before the Neolithic ……….……..30

Enemy images: culture or biology ………..…...…….. 36

War and the culture of war at the dawn of history ………40

    Ancient Mesopotamia
    Ancient Egypt
    Ancient China
    Ancient Greece and Rome
    Ancient Crete
    Ancient Indus civilizations
    Ancient Hebrew civilization
    Ancient Central American civilizations

Warfare and the origin of the state ……..………..….…... 79

Religion and the origin of the state ……..…………....…..83

A summary of the culture of war at the dawn of history . 86

The internal culture of war: a taboo topic ………....… 88

The evolution of the culture of war over the past 5,000 years: its increasing monopolization by the state …... 92

    1. Armies and armaments
    2. External conquest and exploitation: Colonialism and Neocolonialism

3. The internal culture of war and economies based on exploitation of workers and the environment
4. Prisons and penal systems
5. The military-industrial complex
6. The drugs-for-guns trade
7. Authoritarian control
8. Control of information
9. Identification of an "enemy"
10. Education for the culture of war
11. Male domination
12. Religion and the culture of war
13. The arts and the culture of war
14. Nationalism
15. Racism

Summary of the history of the culture of war 176

References ....…....... 181

Index ....…………...…….. 195

INTRODUCTION

There are many histories of war, but since the dialectic concept of culture of war/culture of peace is a new concept, this is the first time that anyone has attempted to write a history of the culture of war. As for the culture of peace, it it too early to write anything but a most preliminary history (See Adams 2003). In fact, as it will be argued later in this book, we should not expect that there will ever be a culture of peace in the framework of the nation-state.

As demonstrated by the Seville Statement on Violence (Adams, 1989, 1991), the institution of warfare and its associated culture of war are not biological phenomena inherited from our primate ancestors; instead they are cultural phenomena. Quoting the great anthropologist Margaret Mead, "The same species who invented war is capable of inventing peace." Therefore it is important to ask what is culture, and how and why the culture of war was invented and has been sustained, i.e. what has been its usefulness?

WHAT IS CULTURE AND HOW DOES IT EVOLVE?

The laws of cultural evolution are similar although not identical to the laws of biological evolution. The best scientific study of this, in my opinion, is by the anthropologist Leslie A. White in his book *The Evolution of Culture* (1959).

> "We may think of the culture of mankind as a whole, or of any distinguishable portion thereof, as a stream flowing down through time. Tools, implements, utensils, customs, codes, beliefs, rituals, art forms, etc., comprise this temporal flow, or process. It is an interactive process:

> each culture trait, or constellation of traits, acts and reacts upon others, forming from time to time new combinations and permutations. Novel syntheses of cultural elements we call inventions..."

> ...The interrelationship of these elements and classes of elements and their integration into a single, coherent whole comprise the functions, or processes, of the cultural system..."

> "For certain purposes and within certain limits, the culture of a particular tribe, or group of tribes, or the culture of a region may be considered as a system. Thus one might think of the culture of the Seneca tribe, or of the Iroquoian tribes, or of the Great Plains, or of western Europe as constituting a system. ... But the cultures of tribes or regions are not self-contained, closed systems in actuality, at all. They are constantly exposed to cultural influences, flowing in both directions with other cultures."

In the present book, the culture of war is considered in the framework of the preceding anthropological analysis: it is a cultural system that has evolved over the flow of time. Although at one time or another, some tribes or regions have been relatively independent from the culture of war, over the course of history most peoples have come under its influence. And, as we shall see, the system of nation-states has been from its beginning embedded within the context of the culture of war.

Also following White's analysis we will see that the various components of the culture of war are all interrelated.

As he says, "It is an interactive process: each culture trait, or constellation of traits, acts and reacts upon others." Hence, to give just one of many possible examples, the secrecy of the culture of war supports authoritarian control by allowing certain information to be held only by those in power, and both make possible the practice of warfare by concentrating the command structure in the hands of a few.

WARFARE IN PREHISTORY AND ITS USEFULNESS

War and the culture of war were invented early in prehistory, but they did not involve slavery or the state, and there was no economy based on exploitation, serfs, etc. or the development of internal repression (the internal culture of war) to maintain the power of a ruling class. And hence the usefulness of war during prehistory was quite different from its usefulness later on after the development of the state, as will be discussed later.

Apparently warfare was widespread by the time of the Neolithic period, judging from archeological data on the extensive fortification of early settlements and the widespread existence of weaponry. Some have argued that warfare was not widespread during human prehistory, based on the fact that ethnographers encountered some non-state peoples that had little experience with warfare. See, for example, the website http://peacefulsocieties.org by B.D. Bonta. At the very least, these data negate the argument that warfare is part of some hypothetical "human nature" (See the Seville Statement on Violence, mentioned above). On the other hand, at least half of the particular societies listed on this website were observed in conditions where warfare was impractical because of extreme environmental conditions and/or populations that were widely scattered or pacified by outside forces. In fact several of the societies on the list (Kung San and Mbuti pygmies) did have historical accounts of warfare at earlier times when their peoples were more numerous and less scattered or were not subjugated by other peoples. For detailed arguments refuting the so-called "peaceful peoples", see Eibl-Eibesfeldt (1979), *The Biology of Peace and War*.

There are so few cases of people without a history of war that when the cross-cultural anthropologists Mel and Carol and Ember set out to examine the ethnographic record for predictors of warfare, "we could not compare societies with and without war to see how else they might differ, because there were too few unpacified societies without war" (quotation from *Making the World More Peaceful* (Ember and Ember 2001)).

We need to distinguish at least two broad periods of prehistory. In the more ancient periods of the Paleolithic and Mesolithic, people maintained themselves by hunting and gathering. The more recent phase of prehistory, corresponding to what archaeologists call the Neolithic, appeared later and was characterized by sedentary agricultural economies with populations sometimes gathered into towns and cities. At the same time, there are some hunter-gatherer societies that persisted through the Neolithic and up until the present time.

As already mentioned, warfare was common during the Neolithic period, according to archaeological data. The excavations of Neolithic cities often show that they were surrounded by walls or palisades that presumably served as defense against enemy invasions or raids. And there is abundant evidence of weapons, including some that would appear to have been specifically designed for use in warfare. More direct evidence is difficult to obtain; indirect evidence includes the account of cranial injuries apparently due to warfare in Schulting and Wysocki (2002), as well as the palisade evidence cited by Milner (1999).

What, then was the usefulness of prehistoric warfare? The most convincing argument, in my opinion, is that prehistoric peoples prepared for warfare so that if they ran out of food, due to natural disaster, they could then raid the supplies of neighboring groups and hence avoid starvation. Let us call this the "raid or starve" hypothesis. This hypothesis is supported by the evidence of cross-cultural anthropology. In their study, *Resource Unpredictability, Mistrust, and War* (1992), the anthropologists Carol and Melvin Ember have shown that the variable that best predicts the frequency of warfare in non-state societies is a history of unpredictable natural disasters. As they explain it in their article *Making the World More Peaceful* (2001):

> "...the fear of unpredictable disasters, rather than actual shortages is what mainly motivates people to go to war. Societies with only the threat of disasters, with a memory of unpredictable disasters during a 25-year period, fought very frequently, just like societies that actually had one or more disasters in the previous 25 years. So we think that people may decide to go to war because they want to cushion the impact of expected but unpredictable disasters, scarcity-producing events they expect to occur in the future but cannot control or prevent. The idea that war is an attempt ahead of time to mitigate the effect of unpredictable disasters is supported by the results pertaining to the outcomes or war. Almost always the victors in war take land or other resources from the defeated, even if the victors do not have resource

problems at the time. If you don't need resources at the time, why take resources from the enemy, if not to protect against anticipated but unpredictable scarcity? Surprisingly, taking resources from the defeated occurs usually in foraging as well as in the agricultural cases. It looks like people even in pre-capitalist societies may have been mainly motivated to go to war for economic reasons."

A second predictor of warfare found by Ember and Ember is the fear that others will attack, which can be explained as the result of frequent warfare in the past. The memory of such warfare would be retained in myth and oral history and would stimulate people to prepare for future wars as well. As to be discussed below, this "preparation" often takes the form of "ritual war" and feuding-type raids.

The "raid or starve" situation would have become especially effective after the invention of agriculture in the Neolithic. In fact, this argument is made in the UNESCO (1994) History of Humanity, Volume I, chapter entitled Overview of From the Beginnings of Food Production to the First States. The author, Sigfried De Laet, describes as follows the transition from hunter-gatherer society to communities with food production in which property impacted on the nature and function of warfare:

> "Property came into existence. No doubt the concept existed in embryonic form among the hunter-gatherers, where each community possessed 'its own' hunting territory. Among farmers, however, the idea of property assumed considerable importance: every farmer had their 'own' fields, their 'own' cattle, their 'own' house and their 'own' tools. At the same time, the other

face of property was revealed, for it led to theft, pillage and also war. A community whose harvest had been destroyed by bad weather would be only too easily tempted to go and plunder the barns of a more fortunate neighbouring village community, but the latter would of course defend its possessions by force. Such wars must have been fairly numerous, as is shown by the fact that most Neolithic villages were fortified ... A class of professional warriors gradually came into being, responsible for defending the village while the farmers and shepherds were in the fields. It may well be imagined that initially all able-bodied men took up arms in cases of danger but that soon a few men were made permanently responsible for maintaining security. Such military activities called for a commander, and this role naturally fell to the village chief, whose powers, as noted earlier, thus took on a military character."

The ethnographic accounts of non-state societies in modern times include many descriptions of their warfare. It may be assumed that the warfare described in these contemporary ethnographic accounts is similar to that of prehistory, and that one can draw inferences from these accounts about the prehistoric culture of war.

An especially detailed analysis of warfare was conducted by a team of anthropologists investigating a village of the Dani in the mountains of New Guinea, a tribe that was relatively uninfluenced by modern civilization. In addition to a monograph by Karl Heider (1979), the expedition produced a remarkable film, *Dead Birds*, which I used to show regularly in my university teaching. As Heider says, "War was an immediate part of Dani life. Every Dani alliance was constantly at war with at least one of its neighboring alliances."

Most of the warfare observed among the Dani did not occur under "raid or starve" conditions, but was instead a kind of ritual warfare. This ritual warfare can be interpreted as practice that keeps the warriors prepared in the case that "raid or starve" conditions should arrive, although this is not perceived as the reason by the participants. Instead, they rationalize warfare in terms of their religious mythology, "to appease the spirits of the ghosts", i.e. their ancestors who have died.

> "The real clue to understanding Dani warfare was the realization that it occurs cyclically in two forms. A brief outburst of violence, the secular phase, sets the political stage for the years-long duration of the routine of the ritual phase of war. We saw only a few months of one ritual phase. The rest of this analysis is reconstruction …"

> "The Ritual Phase of Warfare

> For the five and a half months from early April to mid-September 1961, we were able to observe Dani warfare on the southern front of the Gutelu Alliance where they were engaged with the enemy Widaia. During this time there were nine battles (although two of them never really got going) and nine raids. Six men and boys were killed in the raids. No one was killed in the battles … the Dani say that war is necessary to placate the ghosts …"

"Battles

Battles are formal events involving hundreds of men which take place for a few hours at midday on one of the battlefields in non-man's-land.

Each battle is sponsored by a Big Man in a confederation. He takes major responsibility for what will occur ... The evening before, a Big Man holds a ceremony for his men to prepare for the battle ..."

"By noon the battle is under way, and it will continue in fits and starts for several hours, or until rain has driven the men to cover. At first a few men run toward the enemy, who are still far beyond arrow range. For a few minutes they shout taunts, whoop the *jokoik* cry, wave their weapons and their feather whisks, and then retire. Some of the enemy reciprocate. Gradually the lines get closer together and soon they are within firing range of each other ..."

"Action in battle is constrained in many ways ... Now, I am not suggesting that Dani leaders once sat together in council and forbade fletched arrows, shooting in volleys, tight formations, or guns. Yet if the sole aim of war was killing enemy expeditiously, the Dani could not be considered very skillful. We need to consider war as having many functions, and killing is only one of them.

Raids

"... A raiding party is more often made up of a dozen men from one neighborhood organized by a rising young leader. The men go into raids with no ornaments, moving unseen across the no-man's-land to the edge of enemy territory. They hope to find a careless person alone in a garden or someone coming to the river for a drink, or even to trap a man in a watchtower ... Although the goal of raids is death by surprise, even they are limited by implicit norms. No raids occurred at night ... I think there are no raids at night not because of fear of ghosts but because there are limits to Dani warfare.

The Role of the Ghosts

"... it is the Dani belief in ghosts which keeps warfare going. At the time, when I asked the Dani why they fought, they always said "because of the ghosts." If a man was killed by the enemy, his ghost would lurk around causing various sorts of misfortunes until the people managed to kill one of the enemy in return. Thus, the killing in war, once begun, developed its own internal energy.

The Secular Phase of War

The cycle of Dani warfare is a years-long series of battles and raids between alliances of confederation, broken by a brief outburst of fighting which splits alliances and rearranges the constituent confederations into new alliances, setting the stage for a new series of battles and raids.

During the early 1960's the Gutelu alliance had shown signs of internal stress ... The break finally came in 1966. Before the mists rose on the morning of June 4, hundreds of men of the northern Gutelu made a surprise attack on the nearer compounds of the Wilihiman-Walalua. In an hour they had killed about 125 people and burned many of the compounds..."

"The secular phase of war differs from the ritual phase in many respects: it is rare, it is short, it is very bloody; women and children, as well as men, are killed; property is destroyed and plundered; and it is done for motives of secular revenge."

Although Heider and his colleagues did not observe the Dani under conditions that had deteriorated to the point where they needed to "raid or starve", the 1966 secular phase of war described above corresponds to what one would expect under starvation conditions.

As mentioned, the ritual phases of warfare, battles and raids, are not explained by the Dani as "practice," but instead, they are explained in terms of their beliefs about the role of ghosts. As one watches the filmed accounts of ritual battles the viewer is reminded of modern-day combative sports which have been shown to serve as practice for warfare. Raids are similar to feuding which will be discussed later one as another form of practice.

The distinction between ritual and secular phases of warfare has been made also by anthropologists working in other parts of the world. For example, after reviewing ritual warfare (*tinku*) in the Andes, Arkush and Stanish (2005) conclude that it was related to destructive warfare:

> "To summarize, archaeologists can expect destructive warfare and ritual to go hand in hand. Ritual is also involved in contained forms of festive combat such as *tinku*, games, and rites of passage that can be distinguished precisely by their lack of larger effects. Such setpiece combat surely took place in the prehistoric past, but it should not be associated with fortifications, high rates of trauma, or the other indices of destructive warfare, and we should not be misled by ritual features, trophies, and ritual iconography into thinking that prehistoric conflict was small-scale or unimportant."

The "raid or starve" explanation of warfare is not usually recognized by the peoples who practice it, presumably because the extreme starvation conditions occur so rarely, perhaps only once in many generations. Instead, they may have symbolic explanations like the Danis' ghosts. For the same reason, it is difficult for anthropologists to investigate this hypothesis. Not only are the conditions extremely rare, but even if they were to occur, ethical considerations would impel the anthropologists to intervene and not simply make observations while watching people die of starvation.

Here is a serious weakness of the scientific method, which is good at investigating frequent or easily-repeatable events, but which cannot deal with events that occur only rarely and are not reproducible.

The evolution of traits that are useful only on rare occasions is perhaps easiest to understand in the case of examples from biological evolution, where it is possible to examine hundreds of generations of a plant or animal under relatively controlled conditions. Take, for example, the following discussion of "fire-resistant seeds" in plants, taken from *The Basics of Selection* by Bell (1996).

> *"Selection of Lineages for Specific Adaptation.*
> Any environment is likely to change abruptly at long and irregular intervals; this is part of the variation of the environment on all time scales. Organisms are thus liable to suffer infrequent catastrophes, as the result of the devastation caused by fire, flood, or some similar event. They might become adapted to resist this devastation ... for example, by producing seeds that are able to germinate after fire. If the return time of fires exceeds the lineage scale of the organism, then fire-resistant seeds will not, in most generations, increase the reproductive output of individuals. Such seeds will, rather, affect whether a lineage survives and proliferates... There is, in short, no difficulty in analyzing specific adaptation to rare events in terms of the selection of lineages of appropriate degree.
>
> Any specific adaptation that is favored in this way will be opposed by shorter-term processes. In the first place, it will become degraded by mutation during the intervening period in which it is not being actively maintained by selection; the more extended the lineage, the longer the period involved and the greater the degree of degradation. Second, shorter-term selection

acting through lineages of lower degree may often act antagonistically to longer-term selection... fire resistant seeds, for example, may germinate less easily in normal years, so that selection among lineages, a few generations in extent, is opposed by selection among individuals within lineages. It will, however, by now be a familiar proposition that negative correlation between shorter-term and longer-term fitness will tend to evolve: genes that increase both will be fixed, and those that reduce both eliminated, leaving genes with antagonistic effects segregating in the population."

Now, to understand the usefulness of warfare in prehistory, let us take as a model the preceding description of the evolution of fire-resistant seeds, and substitute "society" for "lineage", "behaviors" for "genes", and "warfare" for "fire-resistant seeds":

Selection of Societies for Specific Adaptation. The environment of any society is likely to change abruptly at long and irregular intervals; this is part of the variation of the environment on all time scales. Societies are thus liable to suffer infrequent catastrophes, as the result of the devastation caused by droughts, floods, or some similar event. They might become adapted to resist this devastation, for example, by developing a culture of war with the military capacity to overcome neighboring tribes and steal their foodstocks or hunting territories. If the frequency of catastrophes exceeds the time scale of several generations, then the coping behavior will not, in most generations, be of evident usefulness. The behaviors will, rather, affect whether the particular society survives and proliferates in the long term. There is, in short, no difficulty in analyzing specific adaptation to rare events in terms of the selection among a number of competing societies.

If the frequency of catastrophes exceeds many generations, then the adaptive usefulness of the behavior itself may be forgotten and may be explained, not in terms of adaptation to catastrophe, but in terms of less specific causes, for example, to appease the spirits of the dead, etc.

Any specific adaptation that is favored in this way will be opposed by shorter-term processes. In the first place, it will become degraded and replaced by competing activities during the intervening period in which it is not being actively maintained by selection; the more extended the society, the longer the period involved and the greater the degree of degradation. Second, shorter-term selection may often act antagonistically to longer-term selection. For example, frequent warfare may kill or injure so many men that a group is less able to grow and prosper than another which engages less in warfare, thus opposing the selection of warfare in all of the societies in a given region. The negative correlation between shorter-term and longer-term fitness will tend to evolve: behaviors that increase both will be fixed, and those that reduce both eliminated. For example, one might expect the behaviors of warfare to become ritualized to the point that the practice is maintained, but the cost of death and injury is minimized.

THE CULTURE OF WAR IN PREHISTORY

The culture of war during prehistory consisted of at least 6 aspects:

1. warriors and weapons
2. authoritarian rule associated with military leadership
3. control of information through secrecy
4. identification of an "enemy"
5. education of young men to be warriors
6. male domination

Weapons and defensive walls are known through archaeological data. Otherwise, we can only assume that the prehistoric culture of war was similar to that found by ethnologists investigating the non-state peoples encountered by European explorers. Most able-bodied men served as warriors. In each tribe they shared a common and unique culture of phrases, gestures, stories, body ornamentation, clothing and skills of weapon-making,, weapon-use and tactics of fighting that distinguished them from the women and from the warriors of other tribes.

The other aspects of the prehistoric culture of war can be reconstructed through cross-cultural analysis of non-state societies by anthropologists such as Carol and Melvin Ember. It is a reasonable assumption that the correlations that they find in the ethnological data of the past few centuries are similar to those that would have existed in prehistoric times.

Authoritarian governance is correlated with warfare frequency. This is measured inversely by Ember and Ember (2001) in terms of checks on leaders' power, ease of removing leaders from power and extensiveness of participation, as described in the following:

> "Because the ethnographic record hardly ever has contested elections or other features of democracy as defined by political scientists, we reformulated our test hypothesis in terms of variables of political life that can be observed and measured universally and reflect a continuum ranging from more to less democracy. Do such variables predict less internal war in the ethnographic record? The answer is yes, and strongly. In multiple regression analyses, three political variables independently and significantly predicted less war within the society: 1) high political participation -- adults participate more in community decisions; 2) peaceful political succession -- there are nonviolent ways to remove leaders; and 3) civil rights -- the community stays together (no fission occurs) after a political dispute, which indicates that people agree to disagree."

Similarly, there is a correlation of warfare frequency with the socialization of young men to be aggressive. This is true for both initiation rites of young warriors, according to Carol and Mel Ember in *War and the Socialization of Children* (2007) and the practice of violent team sports, according to Sipes (1973) (*War, sports, and aggression: An empirical test of two rival theories*). The Embers provide a number of convincing arguments based on data from pacified societies that socialization for aggression is the consequence, not the cause of frequent warfare, in other words, societies with frequent warfare undertake more training of their young men to be warriors. To use their words, "male initiation ceremonies function as the equivalent of basic army training in non-state societies by taking boys or young men away from their families, isolating them from females, and subjecting them to traumatic and grueling conditions".

There are many descriptions of warrior initiation rites. Here are excerpts from a lengthy description by Heider (1979) of one such rite as conducted by the Dugum Dani of New Guinea:

> "The initiation began on the first day of the Pig Feast. About 175 boys, ranging in age from 3 to nearly 20, took part ... The first step was to purify the boys, to remove the effects of all the taboo foods which they had eaten ... The boys' part in the initiation was now suspended for ten days [while] men gathered in a fallow garden to build a compound which they called *Wusa-ma*, the Sacred Place... On the tenth day, early in the morning, the boys were brought to the Sacred Place. Each boy wore an orchid fiber belt and a small red net, and carried weapons [bow and arrows]... As they neared the Sacred Place other men ran ahead to hide in ditches; when the boys approached, they charged forward in noisy ambush... On the second day of their seclusion there was a huge mock battle... [on the final day] they were led single file to a hidden place in a stream bed where a long fire, covered with leaves, smoked away... As each boy arrived he was thrown or pushed into the fire. The screams were horrendous, but

they were screams of surprise, not pain. The leaves dampened the flames, and the boys were well smoked but not burned..."

We will see later on that religion is used by the first empires and states to legitimize the authority of the ruling class and its culture of war, but according to the analysis by Leslie White (1959) in *The Evolution of Culture*, this was probably not the case in prehistoric cultures. As he points out, in prehistoric societies, the gods were invoked to help in the conduct of a war, but not to maintain social control in the society:

> "Primitive peoples negotiate with their gods in order to obtain their good will and help in their struggle for existence with reference both to their natural habitat and to their hostile neighbors. But with regard to their own domestic social affairs, primitive peoples felt for the most part that they could manage them themselves without the interference or the help of the gods... Thus an Indian might seek the aid of spirits in hunting, horticulture, medicine, or warfare, but not in his social relations with his fellow tribesmen. Virtually nowhere do we find that marriage or divorce is an affair of the gods in preliterate systems. Nor is the killing of a fellow tribesman, even a member of one's own family, an affair in which the gods have any concern...
>
> "The late Sir James Frazer has supplied some interesting evidence bearing upon the difference between the ethical systems of tribal societies and those of the higher cultures. Early versions of the Ten Commandments, he points out, have

to do almost wholly with the relationship of man to God, not with man's relationship to man. In one of the early codes which he cities there is not a single ethical commandment, ethical in the sense of governing the relationship of one member of a society to another. Instead, we find rules having to do with religious rituals and sacrifices... In later versions of the Mosaic code, however, we find such commandments as "Thou shalt not steal, commit adultery," etc. Tribal society had by this time been outgrown, and civil society with its state-church had taken its place. Theology had become an instrument of social control."

Although the question of secrecy has not been systematically investigated by cross-cultural anthropology, it is clear from all accounts of non-state warfare that secrecy is essential because the deadly raids of the most serious warfare face the great risk of ambush if their plans are known by the enemy.

In fact, it is the need for secrecy about war plans that can explain the male monopolization and exclusion of women from prehistoric warfare, and the consequent domination by men of all subsequent history.

The culture of war has always been characterized by **male domination**. Where did this come from? My own studies of brain research and animal behavior have indicated that it does not come from men being more aggressive or from any particular difference in the brain of men and women, except insofar as the brain is involved in the determination that only women can bear young (Adams, 1992, *Biology does not make men more aggressive than women*).

The origin of the male monopolization of war is caused by a socio-cultural contradiction rather than biological determinism. This is shown in my 1983 study, *Why There Are So Few Women Warriors* by using statistical analysis of cross-cultural data and predicting the few cases where women warriors have existed.

A woman could not be trusted in war, because her husband would be fighting on one side of the war and her brothers and father on the other side. As mentioned above, secrecy is essential to effective warfare. The danger of women's treachery must have been very frequent in prehistory. This is suggested by the analysis of ethnographic data indicating that most wars were fought between neighboring tribes and communities, and most marriage was arranged so that the wife comes from a neighboring tribe and community and goes to live with the husband (patrilocal exogamy). There was, in effect, a contradiction between the ancient institutions of marriage and war. Under the conditions that were most commonly prevailing (patrilocal exogamy and local warfare) the married woman was caught in a contradiction when there was a war. As mentioned, her husband would be fighting on one side of the war and her brothers and father on the other side.

The simple solution to this contradiction was to exclude women from warfare altogether. In fact, the data support this conclusion, because the only ethnographic reports of women warriors in the sample came from situations when all warfare is against distant enemies with whom one could not inter-marry, or when marriages were arranged inside the community or tribe (endogamy). There were no reported cases of women warriors from tribes with patrilocal exogamy.

The exclusion of women from war had profound implications for all subsequent history as explained in "*Why There Are So Few Women Warriors*" (Adams 1983):

> "Considering all of the foregoing data, it is possible to construct the following hypothesis about the prehistory of warfare. In the beginning, one may suppose, the invention of weapons not only transformed hunting into an especially effective means for getting high-protein food, but it also transformed the noisy, but seldom lethal, territorial displays and attacks against strangers that characterized non-human apes into deadly encounters that could be called true warfare. The distance traveled by hunting and war parties would have precluded the participation of pregnant women or women carrying suckling infants and led to a tendency (not a monopoly) of hunting and warfare by men. The tendency toward a sex role differentiation between male hunting and warfare and female nurturing and gathering of food near a home base may well have provided the material basis for the family unit and the beginnings of marriage. So long as warfare was infrequent, one would have expected such primitive marriage to be agamous and bilocal (i.e. without exclusive exogamy or endogamy and without exclusive patrilocality or matrilocality), like many of today's cultures that have low frequencies of warfare. At this early stage, it should be emphasized, there is no reason to suppose that either hunting or warfare was monopolized by men.

As population density increased and cultures became larger in size, we may suppose that the frequency of warfare increased and that internal warfare came to predominate *[i.e. war was carried out mostly against neighboring groups]*. This would have been associated with restrictions on marital residency so that it was patrilocal and, in many cases, exogamous. Patrilocality may have been necessitated in order to keep young warriors with their fathers and brothers so they could help with the prosecution of the warfare, a proposal made by Ember and Ember (1971). The causal relationship may have been bidirectional since patrilocality is associated with fraternal interest groups which may, themselves, tend to promote internal warfare (Otterbein, 1968). Exogamy may have been instituted in many cases to restrict the ambiguity concerning sexual partnerships. Assuming, as does Divale (1974) that most primitive feuds stem from fights over women, and keeping in mind that under conditions of internal war, men are armed and trained to kill, such ambiguity rises to the level of contradiction. By rigorously instituting marriage and restricting it to exogamy, taking all wives from other communities, the contradiction might be reduced. The relationship of men and women could be clearly specified from the very first time that a woman entered the community through the institution of marriage, each woman "belonged" only to her husband without any prior history or ambiguity to be reckoned with.

With the advent of internal war, patrilocality, and exogamy, there came a profound shift in male-female relations. The male monopolization of warfare was instituted and extended to hunting (in order to preclude the use of weapons by women) and to the initiation rites of the young (male) warriors. The inequality of power between men and women was institutionalized in a way from which we have never recovered. This situation characterizes 35 of the cultures in the present sample, including over half those with large populations."

Looking back at what I wrote in 1983, it is clear that the analysis corresponds fundamentally to the cultural approach pioneered by the anthropologist Leslie A. White (1959) in *The Evolution of Culture.* The evolution of culture is best understood at the socio-cultural level rather than through an approach of biological determinism. Just as White sought to understand the evolution of incest, exogamy and endogamy as socio-cultural solutions to the question of group size and solidarity, so, too, we can best understand the male monopolization of warfare in terms of the socio-cultural solution to the contradiction faced by married women during warfare.

What about the idea that there was widespread matriarchy during prehistoric times and that this was related to a culture of peace? This idea, dating back to Johann Jakob Bachofen (1861), *Mother Right: An Investigation of the Religious and Juridical Character of Matriarchy in the Ancient World,* is still repeated by many contemporary authors, e.g. Elise Boulding (1976) in her otherwise excellent book, *The Underside of History - A View of Women through Time.* I once had the great privilege of exploring with Elise the ancient stone structures in Malta which are often cited as evidence of such a matriarchal period. Indeed, in Malta as in many ancient temple structures, there were images of women which seem to have been worshipped. But Elise could not find a rebuttal to the argument that veneration of the Virgin Mary by contemporary Roman Catholics does not make modern society any less patriarchal. For a time, claims were made that the ancient city of Catal Huyuk, excavated in Turkey, showed signs of having been a matriarchy, since it contained feminine images which seem to have been venerated. However, a further analysis of the data suggested that its culture was a culture of male warriors since men were buried with their weapons and there were fortifications around the city to protect it from warfare.

In general, the consensus among academic specialists is that a strictly matriarchal society never existed. See, for example, the recent book *The Myth of Matriarchal Prehistory: Why an Invented Past Will Not Give Women a Future* by Cynthia Eller (2000).

Once the culture of war was established, it had a profound influence on the **nature of marriage**, which is described above in the excerpt from *Why There Are So Few Women Warriors*. As the frequency of warfare increased during the course of prehistory, it transformed earlier marriage arrangements that had not rigorously specified marital residency (agamous) or had allowed both alternatives (bilocal). At first, when cultural units were small and warfare took place against more distant groups with which there was no inter-marriage (called "external warfare"), there was probably a tendency toward matrilocality. According to the reasoning of Divale in his 1974 paper in Behavior Science Research, *Migration, External Warfare, and Matrilocal Residence*:

> "In the face of severe external warfare, the chances of successful adaptation would be increased if these societies could cease their

> feuding and internal war and instead concentrate all their resources against the other society. Matrilocal residence accomplishes this, because the dispersal of males from their natal villages upon marriage results in the breakup of fraternal interest groups."

Patrilocality became the rule when societies became larger and more complex and warfare took place between groups that also inter-married ("internal warfare"). Under patrilocal exogamy, the marriage partner always came from outside the home village and the couple always took up residence in the village of the man. Based on data from cross-cultural analysis of the ethnographic data from many cultures, Mel and Carol Ember (1971), *The Conditions Favoring Matrilocal versus Patrilocal Residence,* come to the conclusion that patrilocality came into favor because it allowed communities to retain their trained warriors:

> "In short, it appears that whether a society has prevailingly matrilocal or patrilocal residence can be predicted quite handily and reliably from whether it has a pattern of purely external warfare ..."

> "... judging from our data, the fact that warfare is at least sometimes internal appears to require patrilineally related males to be localized after their marriages. Or, in other words, if fighting occurs between neighboring communities, families would want to keep their fighters at home for protection."

An overall survey of the ethnographic literature indicates that marital residency is patrilocal in about 67% of all described societies, reflecting the fact that internal warfare is the more common situation, while it is matrilocal in about 15%, which reflects societies with external warfare. Note that the terms external and internal warfare in the case of anthropological analysis are different from the terms used in contemporary political science, as will be explained later. Most of the remaining 18% of societies have variable arrangements regarding where the newly married couple goes to live, as well as neolocal, living in a new location, and avunculolocal, going to live with the husband's mother's brother.

The culture of war may also have facilitated the prevalence of polygyny, the taking of multiple wives. According to a recent cross-cultural study of this subject, high male mortality in war is the best predictor of polygyny in non-state societies (Ember, Ember and Low 2007). As the authors describe, this confirms and updates an old theory:

> "The 'high male mortality' explanation, first suggested by Herbert Spencer (1876; cf. Carneiro, 1967, p. xliii), is that polygyny develops when there is an excess of females because of high mortality in war .... Consistent with modern theory, we suggest that polygyny is likely to become prevalent if there are more females than males because men who might otherwise not be competitive when women are a scarce resource may be able to marry, and some to marry polygynously."

The correlation of polygyny and warfare does not hold for state societies. The authors suggest that this is because "in nonstate societies most if not all able-bodied men participate in the warfare; [while] in state societies only some men fight because there usually is a specialized or standing army. So high male mortality in war should imbalance the sex ratio more in nonstate societies."

Male dominance has always extended beyond the monopolization of warfare. As mentioned above, it came to include the monopolization of big-game hunting (presumably to preclude the use of weapons by women) and the initiation rites of the young (male) warriors. According to the authoritative survey of Murdock (1937), there are only three exclusively male occupations: warfare, big-game hunting and metal-working. One can make the argument that metal-working was not allowed to women because metal was used primarily to fashion weapons. In contrast, Murdock's survey could not find any occupation that is exclusively female.

Once human societies developed private property, male dominance was extended to property relations. A particularly well-known example is illustrated in the final commandment of the Biblical "Ten Commandments" (note also the mention of slavery as well in this context):

> "Though shalt not covet thy neighbour's house, thou shalt not covet thy neighbour's wife, nor his man-servant, nor his maidservant, nor his ox, nor his ass, nor anything that is thy neighbour's."

In fact, the consequences of the male monopolization of war were so great that one should probably describe prehistoric culture as a ***culture of war and male domination.*** Here it is described by Divale and Harris (1976) in their *American Anthropologist* paper, *Population, Warfare, and the Male Supremacist Complex:*

> "Male dominance is also implicit in the widespread asymmetry of the sexual division of

labor. Women in band and village societies are usually burdened with drudge work, such as seed grinding and pounding, fetching water and firewood, and carrying infants and household possessions. Hunting with weapons is a virtually universal male specialty.

Male supremacy is even more directly displayed in the asymmetry of political institutions. Headmanship occurs widely in band and village societies; headwomanship, in a strictly analogous sense, is no more common than polyandry, if it exists at all. Control over redistributive systems in pre-state societies is seldom if ever vested in women..."

"Central to the sexual distribution of power is the fact that almost everywhere men monopolize the weapons of war as well as weapons of the hunt ... In many band and village cultures women are not even permitted to handle the weapons which males employ in combat ... the combat effectiveness of males is enhanced through their participation in competitive sports such as wrestling, racing, dueling, and many forms of individual and mock combat. Women seldom participate in such sports and to the best of our knowledge, almost never compete with men.

The material, domestic, political and military subordination of women is matched in the ritual and ideological spheres by pervasive beliefs and practices that emphasize the inferiority of females ..."

DATA FROM PREHISTORY BEFORE THE NEOLITHIC

During the Paleolithic and Mesolithic periods before the Neolithic, when people lived by hunting and gathering rather than by agriculture, the data suggest that hunter-gatherers also made war. For a long time it was thought by many anthropologists that hunter-gatherers were more peaceful than agricultural peoples, but that is not supported by cross-cultural analysis. In her study, *Myths About Hunter-Gatherers*, Carol Ember (1978) found that warfare was practiced by 88% of the modern hunter-gatherer societies surveyed, even when excluding equestrian hunters and societies dependent on fishing. The three exceptions are instructive, suggesting that hunter-gatherers did engage in warfare when possible. All three had population densities so low that war was not practical: 1) the Kung bushmen have been decimated over time, but have oral history accounts of warfare in earlier times when they were more numerous; 2) the Yahgan lived under extreme conditions at the southern tip of the Americas and; and 3) the Pekangekun live under similar conditions at the northern extremes of the Americas.

Direct archaeological evidence on the frequency of prehistoric warfare among hunter-gatherers are scant. Since hunter-gatherers did not live in cities, one does not find walls and palisades. There are stone implements that could have served as weapons, but they cannot be definitively distinguished from the weapons used in hunting. Perhaps the best evidence comes from cave and rock-painting by hunter-gatherer peoples. Many of these come from hunter-gatherer peoples who lived during or after the Neolithic, such as those of the African Bushmen illustrated in Eibl-Eibesfeldt (1979), and those of plains Indians of North America at Writing-on-stone in Southern Alberta, Canada, described in *The Archaeology of Rock Art* by

Chippindale and Taçon (1998). In addition, the battle scenes between groups of archers in the cave paintings in Spain, one of which is also illustrated in the Eibl-Eibesfeldt book, previously attributed to the Mesolithic period, are now thought to have been Neolithic.

In the chapter on human violence in the Paleolithic and Mesolithic in Guilaine and Zammit (2001), *Le Sentier de la Guerre,* evidence is drawn from skeletal injuries to suggest that cannibalism was practiced during the Paleolithic among both Neanderthal and Cro-Magnon peoples. As for the Mesolithic, images of figures apparently pierced by spears are shown from cave and rock art in Italy and France, painted over 20,000 years ago. Mesolithic remains of humans apparently killed by spears and arrows are cited from many sites, including in Roumania, France, Algeria, Denmark, Sweden, Russia, Ukraine and India. An especially detailed description is provided of what appears to have been a massacre by spears with stone points of 59 people all ages and sexes at "site 117" near Djebel Sahaba in the Sudan along the Nile River some 12,000 years ago.

Although it appears that warfare took place during the Paleolithic and Mesolithic, we don't know much about it. For example, we do not know at what point in prehistory warfare and hunting were monopolized by men. Perhaps this could be determined by a survey of objects buried with women and men. Was there an early time when women were buried with the weapons of hunting and war? Data are available on women warriors from the Neolithic era such as the Sauro-Sarmation "warrior-women" tomb complexes described by Davis-Kimball (1997), but comparable data do not seem to be available from earlier prehistory.

As discussed earlier, the "raid or starve" explanation is quite plausible for agricultural peoples with stores of food such as those of the Neolithic, but can it explain the earlier warfare among hunter-gatherers? After all, hunter-gatherers would not be expected to have stores of food to the same extent as agricultural peoples. This is not an easy question to answer for several reasons.

First, one should not assume that hunter-gatherers did not store food. Probably they stored less than agricultural peoples, but the difference would have been a matter of degree, not all or nothing.

Second, it is difficult to draw conclusions based on the cross-cultural analysis of contemporary hunter-gatherers or evidence from hunter-gatherers after the beginning of the Neolithic period. One may assume that since the invention of agriculture, many hunter-gatherer peoples have lived in proximity to agricultural people. Under conditions of potential starvation, it would have benefited them to raid the stores of nearby agricultural peoples. This is supported by the statement in a recent review by Roksandic (2004) of violence among prehistoric hunter-gatherers: "For most of these populations, at some point in their history, contact with farming communities was possible even if it did not occur."

Another perspective, preferred by Mel and Carol Ember in our discussions, is that the key moments of the use of warfare to avoid total starvation do not come at the last minute on the verge of starvation, but rather at a point somewhat earlier in time as the hunting and gathering territories yielded less and less under drought conditions and the territories had to be expanded in order to find food and water. At this point, neighboring groups would have come into conflict over their territories and one group might attack the other in order to gain more territory for subsistence. This is also the opinion of Irenaus Eibl-Eibesfeldt (1979) in his book, *The Biology of War and Peace:*

> "The history of mankind down to the present day is the history of the successful conqueror. Whether or not territorial gain plays a part in the subjective motivation of war is a completely secondary question in that respect. What counts is the result..."

> "Although the declared objectives of their wars are to capture women and to show other groups that they are ready to defend their sovereignty by force, nevertheless, the demonstrable result, apart from the capture of women and the gain in prestige, is that the winners often exterminate the losers or force them to abandon territory. It is this result that counts, even though the motivations put forward by those involved are different ... Wright states this clearly: 'The function of an activity may be broader than its intention.'"

> "Wars are fought for hunting grounds, pasture land, and arable land, and if in earlier times, climatic alterations made a group's living area inhospitable, it was actually compelled to find new territory by force of arms."

Much of the armed conflict that has been described among hunter-gatherers is better considered as **"feuding"** rather than warfare. For example, feuding best describes the attacks by one group upon another among the Australian aborigines in the original ethnographic accounts of these hunter-gatherer peoples. These descriptions are particular revealing since the Australian aborigines are a people that had no contact with agriculture or the state prior to the relatively recent arrival of Europeans. Here are excerpts from a description of aboriginal feuding that was observed by Spencer and Gillen (1927) over a century ago and described along with remarkable photographs of the raiding party:

> "During the time that we spent amongst the Arunta at Alice Springs, in the month of May 1901, we were fortunate enough to witness the dispatch and return of another *atninga* or avenging party. Some few months earlier an Alice Springs native had died, and his death was attributed by the medicine men to the fact that he had been killed by the evil magic of a man living some 130 miles away to the north-west. Accordingly, while a large number of men were gathered together, advantage was taken of the occasion to organize an avenging party ... That night was spent in the camp making and singing over the *ilkunta* or flaked sticks which the men were to wear in their hair while on the war-path.
>
> Early the next morning the men, armed with spears, boomerangs, and shields, and wearing the *ilkunta* or flaked sticks, came dancing up the bed of the creek in the form of a solid square ... all the men in camp were gathered together and a series of ceremonies called *atninga unterrima* was performed ... "
>
> "[After the ceremonies] Rising to their feet, each member of the party took his shield, spear, and boomerang, and off they started as cheerfully as if they were setting out upon a pleasure trip..."

"[After their return and special ceremonies to ward off the spirit of the man who was killed] They described how they had found him out in the bush, and had divided into two parties, a larger one of onlookers, or *Alnalarinika,* and a smaller one, *Immiringa,* to do the spearing … It transpired that upon this particular occasion the avenging party had not killed the man whom they actually went in search of. He had somehow got news of their coming, and had discreetly cleared away to a distant part of the country. As they could not kill him they had speared his father, under the plea that the old man had known all about his son "going *Kurdaitcha*" to kill the Alice Springs man, and had not attempted to prevent him from doing so. It will not be very long before a return *atninga* will be organized to visit the Alice Springs group, and then probably the old man's death will be avenged. In this way, year after year, an endless vendetta is maintained among these tribes…"

For another remarkable study of feuding, one is referred to the oral history of feuds over the course of 500-600 years on the South Pacific island of Bellona. This is described by Rolf Kuschel (1989), in his extensive monograph entitled *Vengeance is their Reply*. Kuschel analyses the recollections of people concerning 195 homicides, each one of which was considered to be the cause for vengeance and the succeeding homicide.

What is the usefulness of feuding? Looked at in isolation, it is difficult to explain, but if we consider it in relation to the "raid or starve" hypothesis, it can be understood as practice for warfare. Raids to avoid starvation might occur only once every few generations but when that time came, those social groups that had practiced feuding over the years would be better prepared than other groups that did not practice feuding. In this sense, the usefulness of feuding for hunter-gatherers would be similar to the function of the ritual phase of warfare among the agricultural Dani people in New Guinea as described above.

Once again, we are faced with the gap between explanation of a phenomenon by the participants and its "deep usefulness" in terms of adaptation to rare events. And here again, we see the situation where the "deep usefulness" of warfare in the case of natural disaster and starvation conditions is so rare that participants in feuding behavior may never have experienced it. Instead, the warfare is justified in terms of vengeance against an enemy, and the need to placate the ghosts of the dead. What is this need for vengeance? And is it cultural or biological?

ENEMY IMAGES: CULTURAL OR BIOLOGICAL?

Although the Seville Statement on Violence has shown, through the scientific evidence, that warfare is a cultural and not a biological behavior, there remains another persistent and related question: are enemy images cultural or biological in origin.

This is an important question because we have seen that even the most "primitive" warfare known, the feuding of Australian aborigines, is justified in terms of the vengeance necessary against an enemy. To quote again from the description above: "Some few months earlier an Alice Springs native had died, and his death was attributed by the medicine men to the fact that he had been killed by the evil magic of a man living some 130 miles away to the northwest.... It will not be very long before a return *atninga* will be organized to visit the Alice Springs group, and then probably the old man's death will be avenged. In this way, year after year, an endless vendetta is maintained among these tribes..."

This question is also important because vengeance remains an essential aspect of the culture of war in the contemporary world. Just to cite two recent examples, President George W. Bush invented the excuse that Iraq was preparing nuclear weapons to be used against the United States in order to justify his 2003 invasion of Iraq, and President Lyndon Johnson invented an attack on U.S. naval forces in the Gulf of Tonkin in order to justify his 1965 invasion of Vietnam.

Do other mammals have "enemies" and, if so, are they cultural or biological. This is a question that I have dealt with in my reviews of the brain mechanisms of aggressive behavior (Adams 1979, 2006). It turns out that in most mammals the brain mechanism of offense (angry attack) is triggered principally, although not exclusively by olfactory stimuli. One mammal sniffs another and if the odors are of the same sex and unfamiliar, the attack mechanism is triggered. This mechanism is probably still intact in the human brain and may explain some cases of human fighting related to very intimate behaviors, but that is not the subject of the present book, and it certainly has nothing to do with human warfare.

Long ago, humans abandoned sniffing each other as a means of initiating behavior, and thereby abandoned biological motivations for sexual and aggressive behavior, replacing them with cultural customs and behaviors. Perhaps the most colorful description of this cultural evolution is that of Sigmund Freud (1930) in a footnote to his book *Civilization and Its Discontents:*

> "The organic periodicity of the sexual process has persisted, it is true, but its effect on psychical sexual excitation has rather been reversed. This change seems most likely to be connected with the diminution of the olfactory stimuli ... The diminution of the olfactory stimuli seems itself to be a consequence of man's raising himself from the ground, of his assumption of an upright gait ... The fateful process of civilization would thus have set in with man's adoption of an erect posture...."

Freud based his argument about the process of civilization on the diminished role of olfactory stimuli as a stimulus for sexual behavior, but the argument is equally valid for the diminished role of olfactory stimuli as a stimulus for aggressive behavior.

Non-human primates continue to sniff each other and to engage in sexual and aggressive behavior that is triggered by the perceived odors, but already at a point of evolution millions of years ago, non-human primates began to involve engage cultural as well as biological factors in their aggressive behavior. In particular, non-human primates as well as humans engage in the behavior of punishment, in which the biological behaviors of attack are triggered by cultural phenomena (Adams 1986):

> "The best evidence I know was gathered by Japanese investigators (Imanishi 1957; Kawamara, 1959) of macaque cultural behavior back in the 1950's...."

> "'Among Japanese macaques, the behavior of some monkeys often implies the function of cultural inhibition. Mothers often show such

behaviors to keep their infants away from dangerous objects, and the leaders do this also... At the Minoo Ravine, when I tried to capture monkeys of the B Troop by a trap, the predominant male held back the monkeys from approaching the trap and attacked the individuals that dared to do so. In the Takago-S Troop, we saw some infants trying to get the bait we had prepared for them, and being driven away by the leaders. In such a way, when any danger is likely to be incurred by the youngsters' 'free floating behavior', some controlling actions were exercised to check them.'"

"... What is the value of punishing behavior? Kawamura points out, in the quotation above, that punishment serves to pass on the social knowledge of dangerous situations from one generation to another. The dominant males and the mothers of infants teach the young animals by punishment to avoid certain kinds of behavior or situations.

Punishing behavior differs in a very important respect from the kind of aggressive behavior that we observe in rats, called offense, which is probably homologous. The motivational stimuli for offense in rats consist of attributes of the opponent such as the odors which indicate whether it is male or female, mature or immature, familiar or unfamiliar. But in the case of punishment, we must deal with a completely new kind of motivating stimuli. It is not the stimulus attributes of the opponent, but the behavior of the opponent that elicits the aggressive response. This is a much more sophisticated kind of stimulus than those which operate in the case of the rat."

Ironically, in the paper cited above, I was trying to explain not warfare but the righteous indignation of peace activists. Hence the title of the paper was *The Role of Anger in the Consciousness Development of Peace Activists: Where Physiology and History Intersect*. The paper goes on to consider the origin of the superego which is one of the basic mechanisms for the elaboration of cultural behaviors and which, it turns out, originates from the internalization of aggressive behavior.

For those who wish to find the evolutionary precursors of enemy images in our biological ancestors, I recommend that they begin looking at the origins of cultural rather than biological motivational stimuli, and a good place to begin would be the cultural phenomenon of punishment. To this day when political and military leaders call upon their people to "punish the enemy", they are drawing upon a cultural behavior that is known by almost every human being from experience in their own family.

WAR AND THE CULTURE OF WAR AT THE DAWN OF HISTORY

The earliest known writings, coming from empires that arose more or less independently in the different continents (China, India, Mesopotamia, Egypt, Greece and Central America), paint a picture of a fully-developed culture of war with the following characteristics:

1. armies and armaments
2. authoritarian rule associated with military leadership

3. control of information through secrecy and propaganda
4. identification of an "enemy"
5. education of young men from the nobility to be warriors
6. religious institutions that support the government and military
7. artistic and literary glorification of military conquest
8. male domination
9. wealth based on plunder and slavery
10. economy based on exploitation (slaves, serfs, etc.)
11. means to deter slave revolts and political dissidents including internal use of military power, prisons, penal systems and executions.

I am using Volumes III and IV of the UNESCO History of Humanity (UNESCO 1994) as a basic source at the dawn of history, and looking at the eight major civilizations that invented writing, as follows:

> Middle East cuneiform writing (Sumerian 3000 BC and Akkadian 2500 BC)
> Egypt hieroglyphic and hieratic scripts : 3000 BC
> Chinese idographic script : 2000 BC
> Crete Linear A script : 1700 BC
> Indic script : 400 BC (Indus script, which is much earlier in association with the Harappan Civilization, is not yet deciphered and no long texts have been found. The Rigveda texts are based on oral traditions going back as far as 1400 BC.)
> Early Hebrew script : 1000 BC

> Greek script : 900 BC
> Central America ideographic writing : 700 BC

By depending on written records, we gain our first picture of the culture of war from the time period between 700 and 3000 BC, i.e. between 3,000 and 5,000 years ago. In many cases the quotations speak of warfare itself rather than its culture, but in reading them we will often find mention of various aspects of the culture of war such as authoritarian governance, images of the enemy, economic growth based on exploitation and oppression, etc.

1. Ancient Mesopotamia

Let's begin with the oldest civilization with writing - the ancient civilization of Mesopotamia. The chapter, "From State to Empire" in Volume II of the UNESCO history describes the rise of the state and its culture in this region. Emphasis here, as we will see with other accounts of early empires, is on the function of war to capture slaves, enlarge territory and amass wealth. The functions of war for external defense and internal control are implied but not specifically mentioned. As described here, leadership of the state originates from military leadership.

> "The emergence of 'city-state' ...denotes the beginning of civilization, when the productivity of social labour reached a level at which society could use the surplus produce to maintain a considerable number of people who were not themselves engaged in productive labour, but fulfilled functions of great importance to society: as administrators, warriors, priests and the 'intelligentsia' - scholars, artists, poets and so on ... surplus product could only grow extensively through robbing neighbours,

capturing slaves, enlarging one's territory and so increasing one's population, or else through unequal trade with neighboring peoples. All this could be done only through war, and war now became a constant factor in the life of society.

Imperial peace promoted trade and generally reinforced economic ties, as well as making for a syncretic, super-ethnic culture. Conversely, it was the empire that first gave rise, in addition to the already commonplace distinction between freemen and slaves or, on a broader footing, between citizens and foreigners, to a distinction among freemen in the guise of a difference between citizens and subjects, that is, between conquerors and conquered. This in turn led to the emergence and spread of ethnic warfare which was hitherto virtually unknown...."

"As war grew in importance, the military leader increasingly came to take pride of place and the office was made permanent ... Disposing of a considerable share of the spoils of war and commanding both the temple guard and the levy of citizens, the *lugal* [military leader] concentrated ever greater power in his hands and increasingly pushed such traditional institutions as the council of elders and other offices to second rank. The Sumerian epic poem *Gilgamesh and Agga* tells how ... when the elders counseled submission, Gilgamesh turned to the assembly of the people which called for war and proclaimed Gilgamesh *lugal*; the war ended with the defeat of Kish. Regardless of the historical accuracy of this story, this train of events is emphatically typical of many later

> periods: a successful military commander, drawing on the support of the masses and flouting the traditional authorities (the council of elders *areopagus* or senate) seizes personal power. This is just how the tyrannies arose in Greece and the constant dictatorships, later to become the empire, in Rome."

As described in the chapter of Volume II on Mesopotamia, the emergent state had an economy based on exploitation, with slaves at the base:

> "By the Early Dynastic period, the increased centralization of state power had produced a dependent labour force among temple and palace personnel, along with the slave and semi-free workers who provided services and production to the estates. Individuals of rural communities may also have been recruited for temporary labour on irrigation and construction work, and have been obliged to give tribute to the temple in the form of agricultural produce. These societies thus contained five major classes of people: nobility, among whom were counted royal administrators, merchants and priests; citizens or community members who held private property; clients of the temple or palace, like artisans who temporarily held pieces of property in exchange for craft products; semi-free labourers who received payment by subsistence rations; and slaves, prisoners of war and other indigent members of the community."

In the chapter in Volume II on Economic and Socio-Political Developments there is discussion of the evolving status of warriors and priests and how each of them serves the palace and the king, i.e. the leadership of the state:

> "The centre of society and of the political structure is provided by the 'great organizations,' that is the temples and the royal palaces ... [in the shift to the late Bronze Age] the different specialized groups are mostly dependent on the palace (temples being now economic agencies subordinated to the palace). The proportion is quite different from area to area, but we may guess that 20% of the population was composed of palace dependents, classified in various groups ...The top of the social and economic ranking is occupied by warriors, scribes, priests and merchants ....Besides the chariot warriors, the palace maintains lower-rank military personnel, mainly as guards. ... Priests are generally reduced to the rank of king's dependents "

We know something of military education in ancient Mesopotamia from the extensive library of one of its last rulers, Ashurbanipal (668-627 BC), over 20,000 cuneiform tablets of over a thousand distinct texts. Ashurbanipal describes in his own annals his education in horsemanship, hunting, chariot driving, and soldiering as well as oil divination, mathematics, reading and writing. The following quotation comes from Curtis and André-Salvini (2005):

> "The art of master Adapa I learned - the hidden treasure of all scribal knowledge ... I mounted my horse ... I held the bow. I shot the arrow, the sign of my valour. I threw unwieldy *azmaru*-spears like arrows. Holding the reins

like a driver I made the wheels go round. I learned to handle the *aritu* and heavy *kababu* shields like a fully-equipped bowman."

This was echoed later by the ancient Greek historian Herodotus who said, "The Persians teach their sons, between the ages of five and twenty only three things: to ride a horse, use the bow, and speak the truth."

For a more detailed description of the role of the religion and priests in support of the state and military leader, the UNESCO chapter on the Development of Religion describes how the king came to be considered as divine and sacred:

> "From the beginning of the third millennium BC we find the same form of government from India to the Atlantic both among nomadic peoples and ethnic groups settled in one place: they had at their head a leader who was acknowledged to have divine powers. Historians call this sacral kingship ..."

> "From the fourth millennium BC in Mesopotamia each Sumerian city-state was headed by a leader who was called *lugal*, 'big man', or *ensi*, 'prince-priest'. He was appointed by the god to rule the city and was supposed to live in his temple. Texts describe royalty as power coming from the gods, a tradition passed on to the Semites as it crops up again in Babylon and Assyria, where the kings' names had similar meanings. They derived their power from their enthronement and coronation. An extensive vocabulary referring to divine light and divine splendour was used to describe their attributes.

> Since the king was responsible for building temples, organizing offerings to the gods, worship, sacrifices and feasts, functionaries gradually replace him and various duties were delegated to priests."

The monumental architecture and art of ancient Mesopotamia, as described in the UNESCO History Volume 2, served to portray and aggrandize the military exploits of the leadership of the state:

> "In Mesopotamia, the various arts depict the feats of the monarchs in the hunting and battle grounds. The Stela of vultures is a bas-relief of the victory of the ruler of Lagash in the twenty-ninth century BC. In another bas-relief in the palace of Nimrud, Ashurnasirpal (ninth century BC) is shown laying siege to a city. Two centuries later, and using the same technique Ashurbanipal appears in a hunting scene at his palace in Ninevah."

This description is echoed in Plates 64 and 69 in the UNESCO history, volume 2. Plate 64, the "victory stela" of Narma Sin (2254-2218 BC), shows the king standing upon his vanquished enemies. Plate 69, the so-called "Standard of Ur" (2685 BC), shows elaborate scenes on its two sides, one of peace (a banquet scene) and one of war, including four-wheeled chariots trampling the enemy, spearmen in armor, soldiers carrying axes, and prisoners of war being presented to the king. As for literature, there were important epic poems preserved as clay tablets in the ancient library of Ashurbanipal. Accounts of warfare are included, although the main themes seem instead to be more religious and philosophical, including how a good king should govern.

Considering the oral tradition of epic poetry relating to the god Marduk in ancient Mesopotamia, it is suggested in the UNESCO History section on Oral Traditions and Literature that the great *Creation* epic, probably written at the end of the twelfth century BC, served as a "propaganda instrument for an empire seeking to justify its political and religious expansion."

The male domination associated with the culture of war that was common in prehistory is apparently retained in early Mesopotamia. Although we find no information in Volume II of the UNESCO History, we may assume that the subservience of women in the period from 700 BC to 700 AD, as described in the following excerpt from Volume III, was also applicable to the earlier period.

> "...in all ancient civilizations - women had no political rights, and nowhere were they allowed to reach a social status even remotely comparable to that of free males. Of course it made some difference whether a woman was enslaved, bought or sold on the market, or if she were the wife of a freeman or of a higher ranked member of society. But even in those cases where women enjoyed excellent material conditions in their daily life, they could only exist within the context of a patriarchal system of life. Even in the highest circles, marriage was arranged by the male members of the two families involved, and the sphere of the married woman's activities was restricted to the household. Normally women belonging to the elite groups of society were also excluded from higher education and from participation in the 'Classical cultures' as creative members of the society. In all cultures there were exceptions -

women who gained prominence as artists, writers or scholars - but they mostly were treated as outsiders."

2. Ancient Egypt

The descriptions of ancient Egypt in the UNESCO history are less detailed than those of ancient Mesopotamia, but its culture of war appears to have developed in very similar fashion. For example, the chapter From State to Empire, describes as follows how the country was unified through warfare and ruled by the victors in a vast bureaucratic system considered to be divine:

> "In Egypt the state developed independently ... the wars that ineluctably arose with the beginning of civilization were bound to lead very rapidly to the unification of the entire Nile Valley under a single power ... The exact manner in which a single ruling power arose in Egypt remains unknown, since it took place before 'recorded' history, that is, prior even to the most ancient extant writings. Because autocracy arose so early in such a vast and rich country, the state sector of the economy absorbed virtually all the other sectors ... The Egyptian pharaohs stood at the apex of a vast, ramified and well-organized bureaucratic system that embraced all areas of social life. Their power and ideological roles were so great that they were regarded as rulers by divine right from a very early stage until the end of the existence of ancient Egypt as an independent state."

A visit to the great Cairo museum provides abundant images of the warfare in ancient Egypt, including images of the Pharaoh crushing his enemies underfoot, images of battle, models of military forces marching in formation, and images of lines of prisoners of war chained together presumably on their way to slavery. Some of these are illustrated in the plates of Volume II of the UNESCO history. For example, Plate 22 shows the Narmer Palette, one of the most ancient documents of ancient Egypt dating from around 3000 BC, in which the king is shown holding a mace and striking an enemy whom he holds by the hair. Also shown are stylized figures of enemies decapitated with their heads put between their legs. The treasures of Tutankhamum, dating from about 1340 BC, include remarkable painted scenes that glorify the king as warrior and hunter. On one side of a painted chest the king is shown on his horse-drawn chariot, much larger than any other figure, shooting arrows at enemies who litter the ground in disorder. On the other side a similar design shows the king shooting at wild animals that are wounded and dying.

One of the battles during the reign of the pharaoh Ramsses (1304-1237 BC) is recorded in scenes on temples erected at the time as well as in several papyrus manuscripts, now housed at the Egyptian Museum in Cairo. The manuscripts describe not only details of the military campaign, but also the importance of spies, military reconnaissance and a peace treaty at the end.

The extent to which ancient Egypt was a class-structured society is debated by experts. There is no doubt that ancient Egypt employed prisoners of wars as slaves; for example, the enslavement of the Israelite people as recorded in the Hebrew Bible. However, it is thought that the construction of the pyramids and other great public works was based on a system of serfdom.

Male domination was not as extreme in Egypt as in most other ancient empires. For example, although most of the pharaohs were men, there were a few exceptions, the most notable being Hatshepsut, who led successful military campaigns but later reigned for many years in a time of relative peace. Some Egyptologists believe that the fact that she was a woman was controversial at the time and was connected to the systematic destruction of her monuments and records by succeeding pharaohs. According to an article on the Internet about the status of women in ancient Europe (Johnson 2002), the legal status of women was equal to that of men in ancient Egypt, although their social status was inferior.

> "From our earliest preserved records in the Old Kingdom on, the formal legal status of Egyptian women (whether unmarried, married, divorced or widowed) was nearly identical with that of Egyptian men. Differences in social status between individuals are evident in almost all products of this ancient culture: its art, its texts, its archaeological record. In the textual record, men were distinguished by the type of job they held, and from which they derived status, "clout," and income. But most women did not hold jobs outside the home … But in the legal arena both women and men could act on their own and were responsible for their own actions. This is in sharp contrast with some other ancient societies, e.g., ancient Greece, where women did not have their own legal identity, were not allowed to own (real) property and, in order to participate in the legal system, always had to work through a male, usually their closest male relative (father, brother, husband, son) who was called their "lord." Egyptian women were able to

acquire, to own, and to dispose of property (both real and personal) in their own name. They could enter into contracts in their own name; they could initiate civil court cases and could, likewise, be sued; they could serve as witnesses in court cases; they could serve on juries; and they could witness legal documents. That women very rarely did serve on juries or as witnesses to legal documents is a result of social factors, not legal ones."

The art works of ancient Egypt include victory stela that were made to mark military victories. The victory stela of Merenptah (1237-1226 BC) was made to commemorate Egypt's victory over the Libyan and Proto-Hellenic invaders, whom they called the 'sea people'. On the same stela is also commemorated the Egyptian invasion and destruction of Israel, including the lines, 'Israel is laid waste, its seed exists no more'.

There are extensive records on papyrus from ancient Egypt, including poetry, biography, novels and moral doctrine, as described in the UNESCO history (the Nile Valley (3000-1780 BC) - The riches of the intellect). These include pedagogical texts which are not devoted to military education; but place an emphasis instead on moral education. There are some accounts of victorious military expeditions, and they seem intended to glorify the generals and pharaohs involved.

3. Ancient China

The development of the first empire in China followed a course of war and culture of war that was remarkably similar, although apparently independent, of the earlier empires in Mesopotamia and Egypt. This is described in the section on the Shang Dynasty in the UNESCO history, including the social structures of the culture of war such as slavery, monarchy and male domination:

> "As early as 1600 BC, China entered the Bronze Age, with her oldest civilization coming into being. This civilization founded the earliest state organization, built fortified cities, created a writing system, developed bronze metallurgy and casting, and other cultural innovations. All this happened in the Shang period in China's history ..."
>
> "The Shang dynasty ruled a slave-owning state. As the largest slave owner, the Shang king was always launching wars upon other tribes in order to seize as many captives as possible. Being their owners' tools and property, slaves had to engage in all sorts of productive and domestic work and, moreover, they were often given away as awards and gifts, and even sacrificed as human victims to be buried with their dead owner or offered to gods and spirits in religious ceremonies. In the royal burial area of the Yin ruins, numerous sacrificial pits arranged regularly have been uncovered, each containing about a dozen headless skeletons, the remains of human victims in successive memorial ceremonies to the departed Shang kings. According to statistical data, the Yin ruins have yielded human victims totaling over 2,300 ... such large-scale slaughter reflects the slave-owning nature of Shang society.

> The Shang state was a monarchy, with the king holding sovereign power and governing the aristocracy, consisting of the chiefs of numerous tribes ... Men held the dominant position in the family, though women enjoyed a few social rights as well ..."

The subservience of women in ancient China is illustrated by the following excerpt from a poem by Fu Xuan in the Third Century BC:

> "How sad it is to be a woman!
> Nothing on earth is held so cheap.
> Boys stand leaning at the door
> Like Gods fallen out of Heaven.
> Their hearts brave the Four Oceans,
> The wind and dust of a thousand miles.
> No one is glad when a girl is born:
> By her the family sets no store.
> Then she grows up, she hides in her room
> Afraid to look a man in the face.
> No one cries when she leaves her home--
> Sudden as clouds when the rain stops.
> She bows her head and composes her face,
> Her teeth are pressed on her red lips:
> She bows and kneels countless times.
> She must humble herself even to the servants."

It is not clear from the UNESCO history to what point various social classes, other than masters and slaves, were distinguished during the Shang Dynasty, although in the succeeding dynasty in China, the Western Zhou Dynasty (1027-771 BC), it was certainly developed:

> "The king and vassals controlled a whole set of bureaucratic apparatus, which managed daily

> governing affairs according to the wills of the rulers. Among the ruled there was the plebeian class who cultivated the 'private field' under the *jing-tian* system and had to work in the 'communal field' for the feudal lord; still they managed to keep their freeman status. At the bottom of society were slaves who had lost their personal liberty."

According to the UNESCO history, it was not until the Western Zhou Dynasty that religion came to fully support the culture of war:

> "Some new religious ideas, for instance, the concept of the Supreme God (Shang-Ti), came into existence. The Supreme God was believed to be the sovereign dominating all other gods, and it was he who granted the 'mandate of the heaven' to the kings and entrusted them with the power of ruling the world. Such use of religious ideas for maintaining the dynasty's domination was a new development."

Did the arts glorify the culture of war in ancient Chinese civilizations? One can point to the recently-discovered life-sized terracotta soldiers buried during the Qin Dynasty around 207 BC, which was the period during which the Great Wall of China was completed. However, this spectacular finding was not necessarily pertinent to the everyday culture of the period, since it was buried with the emperor. From the earliest dynasties, Shang and Western Zhou, there are paintings and murals, but again they do not seem to have been designed to glorify the culture of war.

Important manuscripts have been preserved from the Western Zhou Dynasty, including the *I Jing* (divination manual), the *Shi Jing* (Book of Odes) and the *Shu Jing* (Book of Documents). The latter includes many documents relating to warfare, such as "the speech at the battle of Gan," "The punitive expedition of Yin", "the successful completion of the war on Shang", although the essential themes of these manuscripts seemed to have been more philosophical, laying the basis for the ideology of Confucius (551-479 BC).

Sun Tzu's Art of War dates from the time of Confucius. This book on military strategy and tactics has been very influential throughout Chinese history and is still respected by military minds today, having been used extensively by Mao Tse Tung. An English translation of the full text of its 13 chapters is available on the Internet at http://www.chinapage.com/sunzi-e.html

Sun Tzu emphasizes the importance of warfare to the state and of authoritarian control to the culture of war. He begins as follows with a phrase that sums up the most important message of the present book:

> "The art of war is of vital importance to the State. It is a matter of life and death, a road either to safety or to ruin. Hence it is a subject of inquiry which can on no account be neglected.
>
> The art of war, then, is governed by five constant factors, to be taken into account in one's deliberations, when seeking to determine the conditions obtaining in the field. These are: (1) The Moral Law; (2) Heaven; (3) Earth; (4) The Commander; (5) Method and discipline.
>
> The Moral Law causes the people to be in complete accord with their ruler, so that they

> will follow him regardless of their lives, undismayed by any danger.
>
> Heaven signifies night and day, cold and heat, times and seasons.
>
> Earth comprises distances, great and small; danger and security; open ground and narrow passes; the chances of life and death.
>
> The Commander stands for the virtues of wisdom, sincerely, benevolence, courage and strictness.
>
> By method and discipline are to be understood the marshaling of the army in its proper subdivisions, the graduations of rank among the officers, the maintenance of roads by which supplies may reach the army, and the control of military expenditure."

Of special interest to our thesis are Sun Tzu's assertions on control of information, in particular the role of secrecy and surprise:

> "All warfare is based on deception.
>
> Hence, when able to attack, we must seem unable; when using our forces, we must seem inactive; when we are near, we must make the enemy believe we are far away; when far away, we must make him believe we are near.
>
> Hold out baits to entice the enemy. Feign disorder, and crush him.

If he is secure at all points, be prepared for him. If he is in superior strength, evade him.

If your opponent is of choleric temper, seek to irritate him. Pretend to be weak, that he may grow arrogant.

If he is taking his ease, give him no rest. If his forces are united, separate them.

Attack him where he is unprepared, appear where you are not expected.

These military devices, leading to victory, must not be divulged beforehand."

4. Ancient Greece and Rome

The culture of war in ancient Greece was similar in most respects to what we have seen in other parts of the world at that time, as we know from their epic poem, the Iliad and from the earliest history books, such as the Peloponnesian Wars written by Thucydides. As is stated repeatedly in the Iliad, although the ostensible reason for the war was to recover the beautiful Helen, the taking of plunder and slaves was always assumed.

In describing the history of Greece (Hellas) Thucydides emphasized the role of warfare, beginning with the Trojan War:

> "... Before the Trojan war there is no indication of any common action in Hellas... [Leading up to the war] the coast populations now began to apply themselves more closely to the acquisition of wealth, and their life became more settled;

some even began to build themselves walls on the strength of their newly-acquired riches. For the love of gain would reconcile the weaker to the dominion of the stronger, and the possession of capital enabled the more powerful to reduce the smaller towns to subjection. And it was at a somewhat later stage of this development that they went on the expedition against Troy..."

"[After the Trojan war] ... as the power of Hellas grew, and the acquisition of wealth became more an object, the revenues of the states increasing, tyrannies were by their means established almost everywhere, - the old form of government being hereditary monarchy with definite prerogatives, - and Hellas began to fit out fleets and apply herself more closely to the sea.... "

"But at last a time came when the tyrants of Athens and the far older tyrannies of the rest of Hellas were, with the exception of those in Sicily, once and for all put down by Lacedaemon ..."

"Not many years after the deposition of the tyrants, the battle of Marathon was fought between the Medes and the Athenians ... the whole period from the Median war to this, with some peaceful intervals, was spent by each power in war, either with its rival, or with its own revolted allies, and consequently afforded them constant practice in military matters, and that experience which is learnt in the school of danger ..."

> "The Median war, the greatest achievement of past times, yet found a speedy decision in two actions by sea and two by land. The Peloponnesian war was prolonged to an immense length, and long as it was it was short without parallel for the misfortunes that it brought upon Hellas. Never had so many cities been taken and laid desolate ... never was there so much banishing and blood-shedding ..."

The ancient Greek economy was based on slavery. Whether other social classes were exploited as well is a matter of debate. In one recent scholarly paper, *Class, Embeddedness and the Modernity of Ancient Athens,* Mohammad Nafissi (2004) cites Aristotle as witness to class conflict between the rich and poor freemen at that time:

> "What really differentiates oligarchy and democracy is wealth or the lack of it. It inevitably follows that where men rule because of the possession of wealth, whether their number be large or small, that is oligarchy and when the poor rule, that is democracy. . . But the same people cannot be both rich and poor, and this is why the prime division of a state into parts seems to be into poor and the well-to-do. Further owing to the fact that the one group is for the most part numerically small, the other large, these two parts appear as opposites among the parts of the state. So the constitutions are accordingly constructed to reflect the predominance of one or the other."

The culture of war of the first empires exploited not only people but also the environment. This is an aspect of the culture of war that has received more attention in modern times but which already existed at the time of the ancients. For example, if one goes to Sicily one will find Roman mosaics portraying a land of deep primeval forests filled with big game including lions. But the forests were destroyed by the Romans in their insatiable need for timber for ship-building and wooden houses, and what the Romans did not destroy, the Arabs did later in exploiting the timber for their own ships. There is a great contrast between the scenery in the Roman artwork and today's Sicily which has never recovered its forests.

The subservient status of women in ancient Greece and Rome is especially important because it set the stage for the continued inequality between men and women in Western society down until the present time. This is described in Volume III of the UNESCO history:

> "It is sometimes said that the Greek city was 'a men's club, made by men for men...'"

> "Women occupied a clearly defined place in the civic community, assigned to them by institutions and, above all, by men's conception of their role. They enjoyed none of the political privileges that went with citizenship, taking no part in the assemblies, the courts or the magistracy ... Nor did they play a part in the defence of the city, other than in exceptional circumstances when it was besieged and the entire population joined in its defence. Otherwise, their contribution to the war effort is only to be found in the mental constructs of the philosphers or in the mythical universe of the Amazons, a product of male fantasy."

In Rome, as it had been in Greece, property usually belonged to men and not women, as described by Suzanne Dixon (1985) in The American Journal of Philology, *Polybius on Roman Women and Property*:

> "The essence of the woman's position in Roman law was that she could never technically become a free agent. ... males remained *in patria potestate* until the death of their fathers, when they became *sui iuris*, able to own and dispose of property in their own right. Daughters, too, became *sui iurzj* in these circumstances, but they acquired a *tutor* whose permission *(auctoritas)* was required for major pledges or transfers of property, such as the promise of dowry or making a will. Male children were subject to such a restriction until the age of fourteen, but women *sui iuris* required a *tutor* (or *tutores*) for life. ... The Roman notion of family-based property ownership underpins this system. The *paterfamilias* was the only person in his immediate family with full legal rights to own and dispose of property."

The extensive military writings of the Greeks and their successors, the Romans, are especially well-known and they give us many detailed insights into the culture of war. For example, they provide information in detail on military education and on the control of information; secrecy and propaganda in early civilizations.

The system of education in ancient Greece was intended to train soldier-citizens. This is described in Volume III of the UNESCO history in the chapter entitled, *The Polis in Classical Times*:

> "... most of the cities took considerable care to prepare young people for their responsibilities as citizens. In Sparta this preparation, known as *agoge*, took the form of education, by the state, of youths from early childhood until manhood. Characterized by strict discipline, collective events and activities, and initiation rites throughout the various stages of their education, this system was intended to train soldier-citizens accustomed to living together and imbued with loyalty to the community. The men educated in this way became citizens who were remarkably effective in defending the city and maintaining the established social order. Among the Athenianns, the education of children remained a family affair, but youths of 18 to 20 - the *ephebes* - were given special attention by the city authorities. The education of the *ephebes*, who were registered as citizens at the age of 18, included military training during which they learnt to handle weapons and carry out garrison duty in the small fortresses strung across the territory."

The best known example of the training of warriors in ancient Greece is the Olympic Games. In his *Memorabilia*, the Greek soldier and writer, Xenophon, recalls the remarks of the great philosopher Socrates (who himself had competed in the games as a young man) to one of his young students, Epigenes, on the importance of the Games for physical training and preparation to be a warrior:

> "'You need physical training just as much as those intending to compete at Olympia; or does the life and death struggle with their enemies which the Athenians will undertake someday

seem of small importance to you? Indeed, many men die amid the dangers of war or are saved in some disreputable fashion because of their bad physical condition. Many are captured alive for this very reason, and if this happens to them spend the rest of their lives in the harshest slavery..."

Warriors need constant training and practice in the arts of war, as well as basic physical training. There is a remarkable reference to this for the Roman army as described by the Greek writer Arrian in his book *Tactica*. After describing in some detail the training of cavalry, he concludes that they need to practice the techniques of the best armies in history:

"All these exercises have been understood by the Roman cavalry and have long been practiced. The emperor indeed seeks out foreign practices with which to train them, for example the manoeuvres of the horse-archers of the Parthians and Armenians, the wheeling and revolutions practiced by the lance-bearing cavalry of the Sarmatians and the Celts... To sum up, of the ancient exercises there is none that the Roman have omitted and not practiced from the beginning. Of the other exercises that the emperor has discovered, some contribute beauty, some speed, some inspire terror, and some provide whatever is needed for the job in hand."

As for control of information and secrecy, Thucydides mentions surprise attacks no less than 16 times in his history of the Peloponnesian War. In fact, the element of surprise (and the need for secrecy) has been critical to successful warfare from the beginning of war in prehistoric times, as we have seen in the ancient Chinese text, Sun Tzu's *Art of War*, and it is no less important today.

A corollary to the importance of military secrecy is the phenomenon of "treason" - the betrayal of secrets. Thucydides, for example, describes one such case of treason and the success of surprise attack:

> "The weather was stormy and it was snowing a little, which encouraged him [Brasidas] to hurry on, in order, if possible, to take every one at Amphipolis by surprise, except the party who were to betray it. The plot was carried on by some natives of Argilus, an Andrian colony, residing in Amphipolis, where they had also other accomplices gained over by Perdiccas or the Chalcidians. But the most active in the matter were the inhabitants of Argilus itself, which is close by, who had always been suspected by the Athenians, and had had designs on the place. These men now saw their opportunity arrive with Brasidas, and having for some time been in correspondence with their countrymen in Amphipolis for the betrayal of the town, at once received him into Argilus, and revolted from the Athenians, and that same night took him on to the bridge over the river; where he found only a small guard to oppose him, the town being at some distance from the passage, and the walls not reaching down to it as at present. This guard he easily drove in, partly through there being treason in their ranks, partly from the stormy state of the weather and the suddenness of his attack, and so got across the bridge, and immediately became master of all

the property outside; the Amphipolitans having houses all over the quarter."

Of course, propaganda was used throughout ancient civilizations as reviewed in the following description carried by Wikipedia on the Internet:

"Propaganda has been a human activity as far back as reliable recorded evidence exists. The Behistun Inscription (c. 515 BC) detailing the rise of Darius I to the Persian throne, can be seen as an early example of propaganda. The Arthashastra written by Chanakya (c. 350 - 283 BC), a professor of political science at Takshashila University and a prime minister of the Maurya Empire, discusses propaganda in detail, such as how to spread propaganda and how to apply it in warfare. His student Chandragupta Maurya (c. 340 - 293 BC), founder of the Maurya Empire, employed these methods during his rise to power. The writings of Romans such as Livy (c. 59 BC - 17 AD) are considered masterpieces of pro-Roman propaganda."

5. Ancient Crete

The Minoan civilization on Crete which lasted about 600 years following 2000 BC, took a course quite different from other civilizations, prompting speculations that their culture was more like a culture of peace than a culture of war. According to the section on The Aegean World in the UNESCO history, there were no fortifications and no glorification of war :

> "In the second millennium BC there were no fortifications in Crete, and the Minoan iconography depicts neither scenes of war nor even warriors [*Note added by editor: extensive fortifications have been found in more recent excavations.*] What is more, neither the graves nor the other Cretan environments of the time have yielded any weapons. However, the recollection of a Minoan thalassocracy [empire of the sea] was perpetuated in the traditions handed down to the Greeks by the Cretans. It is consequently assumed that an understanding prevailed among the Minoan states and that they were afforded protection against any seaborne attack by their fleet or that of their allies. This situation has been termed the *pax minoica*."

As mentioned earlier, there is a strong causal relation between the culture of war and the status of women. In this regard, it seems appropriate that the status of women in ancient Crete was more equal than that of women in other ancient civilizations. For example, it is remarkable that it is a woman who is leaping over the bull in the wall painting illustrated in Plate 49 in the UNESCO volume. According to the preceding source, women played important social roles:

> "Cretan women took part in social and religious events and, furthermore, played an important part in society. It would, however, be rash to conclude from this that Cretan society was matriarchal ..."

Similarly, the state appears to have been less authoritarian than in other ancient civilizations. The role of the king was unlike that on the Greek mainland where "the

Mycenean king, or annex, was required to be a great warrior" ...

> "In the Minoan states, the king is thought to have performed the functions of priest and judge but did not wield power of any note in other matters."

In general, according to the UNESCO history, the Cretan civilization was peaceful compared to that on the mainland of Greece which, like other empires in the ancient world, was a culture of war.

> "The rich repertoire of the wall paintings is an inexhaustible source of information on the flora, the fauna and the environment of the period, the dress, hairstyles, and various - economic, social, religious - activities of the inhabitants of the Aegean. Through these wall paintings the different nature of the worlds, the Minoan and the Mycenaean, emerges: that of Crete and the islands is peaceful and happy, that of the Greek mainland martial and harsh."

The civilization of Ancient Crete did employ some slaves, although it appears that unlike in other empires, they were obtained through trade rather than military conquest. Slaves are not mentioned in the UNESCO history. However a search of literature on the subject reveals that slaves had more freedom than in other empires. The Gortyn Laws (about 450 BC) that have been preserved as stone inscriptions in Crete make reference to rights of marriage and property: "XI. If a slave going to a free woman shall wed her, the children shall be free; but if the free woman to a slave, the children shall be slaves; and if from the same mother free and slave children be born, if the mother die and there be property, the free children shall have it; otherwise her free relatives shall succeed to it."

The roles of master and slave were reversed during the Hermaia festival in Crete as inscribed on an ancient altar and described on the Kairatos Internet site (see references). "In the Hermaia festival the slaves were enjoying in the houses of their masters, and the masters had to serve them. At first, this was ritual procedure, but later it became custom and part of the tradition." And according to Versnel (1990), "Ephoros even knows of a festival in Kydonia on Crete where the serfs, the Klarotes, could lord it in the city while the citizens stayed outside. The slaves were also allowed to whip the citizens, probably those who had recklessly remained in the city or re-entered it."

6. Ancient Indus civilizations

We know something of the culture of war in the ancient civilizations of the Indus valley from the hymns of the Rigveda which apparently were composed orally beginning as early as 1400 BC. As described in the chapter on The Post-Indus Cultures in Volume II of the UNESCO history:

> "The king was pre-eminently the war lord and the *Rigveda* gives some idea of the mode of warfare. The king and his nobles fought from chariots and the common people on foot. As in later days, we hear of martial music and banners in connection with battle. The principle weapon was the bow and arrow. The arrows were tipped with points of metal or poisoned horn. Other weapons were lances, spears, axes, swords and sling stones. The king was assisted by two assemblies called *sabha* and *samita*. Great

> importance was attached not only to concord between the king and the Assembly but also to a spirit of harmony among the members of the Assembly. A hymn of the *Rigveda* invokes such a unity: 'Assemble, speak together, let your minds be all of one Accord.'
>
> The royal authority was to some extent curbed by the power and prestige of the priest (*purohita*) who accompanied the king to battle and helped him with prayers and spells."

The culture of war must identify an enemy and that is specifically described in the Rigveda:

> "The despicable enemies who dare deny Indra's supremacy are referred to as *dasa* or *dasyu*. They have a black complexion, flat noses and they are indifferent to the gods. They do not perform the Aryan sacrifices and probably worship the phallus. But they are wealthy with great stores of gold and live in fortified strongholds."

It is not clear from this if the *dasa* or *dasyu* were themselves enslaved but in any case, slavery was practiced at the time according to other verses in the Rigveda.

A religious renunciation of the culture of war by an emperor, relatively unique in history, occurred in the Maurya Empire of the Indian sub-continent in the Third Century B.C. The emperor Ashoka renounced his earlier military exploits and adopted the non-violence of the Buddhist religion for his kingdom. Quoting from Volume III of the UNESCO History of Humanity:

> "After witnessing massacres during a campaign in Kalinga (present Orissa), Aśoka gradually became an enthusiastic supporter of Buddhism. The king subsequently had a great number of rocks and pillars inscribed with his messages of peace and tolerance, which were the basis of his ideology described as *Dhamma*. This term, the Prakrit equivalent of Sanskrit *Dharma*, variously translated as Virtue, Sacred Duty and Social Order, was used for Aśoka's ideology, actually a system of social responsibilities including loyalty towards elders, concern for the sick and respect for *Brahmanas* and *Samanas* as well as many other duties."

The UNESCO history also provides details of an earlier, less highly-developed civilization in the Indus Valley that apparently did not have a culture of war. It has been called the Harappan civilization, named after one of its large cities that has been excavated. According to available evidence, this civilization did not have warfare, nor did it develop a state structure like most of the others mentioned above. Yet it was a complex civilization, as described by Thomas J. Thompson (2006) in *An Ancient Stateless Civilization: Bronze Age India and the State in History:*

> "The people of this civilization used writing, at least for limited purposes (the Harappan writing system, available only in short inscriptions, is as yet undeciphered), made extraordinarily widespread use of metal tools (Shaffer 1982, 46-47), and inhabited a number of *commercial* cities that achieved considerable scale (the five largest had peak populations in the tens of thousands) and remarkable levels of urban amenity (virtually *every* house had a bath

connected to a municipal drainage system). The similar layouts and similar public buildings of Harappan cities strongly suggest that no one of them served as a capital."

According to Thompson, "Harappan remains indicate that neither war nor threats of war played an important part in intercity relations." There were no memorials to military campaigns, little in the way of weaponry and no defensive armor despite the use of metal tools, and walls that did not seem to be designed for military defense but only to charge fees for access to the city. Thompson notes that "of course, it is conceivable that Harappan military science, including logistics and planning, simply did not evolve over a period of seven hundred years to the point that setting a large city to siege was a practical option, but, if so, that fact in itself would be significant."

Although its cities were quite large and there was extensive agriculture, commerce and trade, we don't know much about other aspects of the Harappan civilization since its writing has not been deciphered and it left little in the way of artwork or public monuments. The writing consists largely of seals attached to bundles of trade goods.

7. Ancient Hebrew civilization

The ancient culture of war is known best by many from reading the Hebrew Bible. The books of Exodus and Numbers describe how the Israelites escaped from Egypt and after long wanderings, under the leadership of Moses and the "command" of their god, they conquered the peoples and occupied the "land of Canaan." As part of this campaign, the Israelites conquered the walled city of Jericho, which we know from archaeology as one of the most ancient of all walled cities, dating from before 10,000 BC, long before the earliest empires of which we have record. The account in the book of Joshua of the siege and destruction of Jericho is especially interesting because it illustrates an important and recurring theme in the culture of war, the betrayal of one side in a war by a woman:

> "They took the city ... and destroyed with the sword every living thing in it--men and women, young and old, cattle, sheep and donkeys. Joshua said to the two men who had spied out the land, 'Go into the prostitute's house and bring her out and all who belong to her, in accordance with your oath to her.' So the young men who had done the spying went in and brought out Rahab, her father and mother and brothers and all who belonged to her. They brought out her entire family and put them in a place outside the camp of Israel. Then they burned the whole city and everything in it, but they put the silver and gold and the articles of bronze and iron into the treasury of the Lord's house. But Joshua spared Rahab the prostitute, with her family and all who belonged to her, because she hid the men Joshua had sent as spies to Jericho."

At a later time, as described in the books of Samuel, the celebrated warrior David became the King of Israel, following his victory in what amounted to a civil war with the forces of the previous ruler, King Saul. The Bible describes the exploits of King David and King Solomon, his son and successor, in a way typical of the leaders of ancient civilizations, emphasizing their victorious military campaigns and the building of the great temple. In addition, King David is renowned for his poetry, the Psalms, and King Solomon for his wise judgments. Among King David's poetry is thanks to God for his help in battle:

"It is God who arms me with strength and makes my way perfect. He makes my feet like the feet of a deer; he enables me to stand on the heights. He trains my hands for battle; my arms can bend a bow of bronze. You give me your shield of victory, and your right hand sustains me; you stoop down to make me great. You broaden the path beneath me, so that my ankles do not turn. I pursued my enemies and overtook them; I did not turn back till they were destroyed. I crushed them so that they could not rise; they fell beneath my feet. You armed me with strength for battle; you made my adversaries bow at my feet."

The Bible includes many references to slavery, including the following from the laws in the book of Leviticus: "If a man beats his male or female slave with a rod and the slave dies as a direct result, he must be punished, but he is not to be punished if the slave gets up after a day or two, since the slave is his property." And slaves were taken in the wars such as those of King Solomon as described in the 9th Chapter of I Kings:

"Here is the account of the forced labor King Solomon conscripted to build the Lord's temple ... All the people left from the Amorites, Hittites, Perizzites, Hivites and Jebusites (these peoples were not Israelites), that is, their descendants remaining in the land, whom the Israelites could not exterminate--these Solomon conscripted for his slave labor force, as it is to this day. But Solomon did not make slaves of any of the Israelites; they were his fighting men, his government officials, his officers, his captains, and the commanders of his chariots and charioteers."

As mentioned previously, the male domination of the Hebrew culture of war is expressed, in addition to their use of slaves, in the final commandment of the Biblical "Ten Commandments"

8. Ancient Central American civilization

Mayan writing on public monuments gives us some idea of the culture of war that arose independently in the New World. As described in the chapter on languages in Volume III of the UNESCO history, these monuments may be considered as "political propaganda":

> "Subject matter on the public monuments is very clearly political in nature and, combined with the iconography represented in sculpture, had as its major purpose the recording of the life crisis events of kings and to a certain extent their exploits. Much of what we find on Maya monuments is clearly meant as political propaganda and must be read with considerable caution. Occasionally the focus of the inscription is the military successes of kings, very often involving the capture and the sacrifice of people of high rank from neighbouring states, either warriors, nobles or even kings ..."

We may assume that the educational system of the Mayans was confined to young men and prepared them to be part of the culture of war, although it is not specifically stated in the following description from the preceding source:

> "Some architectural remains in a number of Maya sites suggest that there were special schools in the centres for the noble class, somewhat comparable to the Aztec *Calmecae*. In all probability there were also rural schools among the Lowland Maya somewhat comparable to the Aztec *Telpochcalli*. What we suspect is that general elements of iconography, expressed in public monuments in Classic Maya centres, were understood by virtually the entire population, otherwise their public expression makes little sense. Their purpose is to constantly remind the subjects of the Maya kings of the unusually high status and political and religious privileges of the ruler and of other high ranking individuals. A full understanding of the writing system, however, was probably limited to a small percentage of the population of a Classic Maya realm, probably less than 5 percent and including only the adult males of the noble class."

Further details about the ancient Mayan civilization may be found in UNESCO history description of this civilization during its Classic period. Unlike the great empires in the Old World, it would seem that the rulers commemorated on the public monuments were "rulers of small polities, which even in the Classic period rarely covered more than 2000 square kilometers ..." The rulers were military, political and religious leaders:

> "The Classic period is formally defined as beginning in AD 250, with the first public monumental inscriptions in Maya hieroglyphic script ... Sometimes warfare was for territorial aggrandizement ... Sometimes warfare was for

> general aggrandizement, and large polities were formed temporarily with populations up to 400,000.
>
> Copan has a documented dynasty of at least sixteen rulers between AD 435 and 810 ... Sculptures of subordinate nobles from different parts of the valley suggest that power was being shared, and that each part of the Copan polity was represented in council ..."
>
> "Social ranks can be adduced on the basis of texts, iconography, archaeological evidence and judicious analogies with colonial Maya social structure ... The ruler was war leader, chief protagonist in ritual and the link with the cosmos and the venerated ancestors of the community."

Although the UNESCO history mentions several times the taking of captives in the war by pre-colonial Mayan civilization, it does not mention slavery. However, a source on the Internet (data of which I have not been able to independently verify) indicates that "Slaves did the hard labor in the fields and in construction." [http://history-world.org/maya.htm]. The same source indicates that the status of women was subordinate:

> "Mayan women were respected and sometimes honored, but they exercised their limited freedoms within the bounds permitted by a culture characterized by male domination. As keepers of households and experts in handicrafts, they did all of the weaving and alone produced the highly artistic pre-wheel pottery, for which the Mayans are famous. In performing such important roles, Mayan women

> earned a modicum of respect and status. When a maiden married, her husband came to live in her family's house until he proved himself. She could divorce him and marry again, if she waited a year. She was also permitted to hold property. In many other ways, however, Mayan women were subordinated. They were prohibited from looking directly at men; they waited on men at meals, eating later with other women; and they could not hold public office or enter a temple. Those in elite or royal families were regularly exported for marriage into foreign families, serving as political trade goods for cementing alliances or clinching trade agreements."

The themes of art and religion in the Mayan civilization appear to have served the culture of war. Among the most remarkable artistic productions were the Olmec colossal heads, which, according to the UNESCO history, may have be meant to glorify the leadership of the state:

> "Since these figures do not represent gods - for they lack the distinguishing characteristics and symbolic signs which might allow such an interpretation - they may rather depict 'lineage leaders' or 'ancestors'. Such representations would be justified in a society which, an all probability, was politically organized into various chieftainships ..."

> "All this, in conjunction with the development of temple-like architectural forms, points sharply to the existence of a solid religious system, one implying a state-like political organization, going beyond that of mere chieftainship or headmanship; one indeed, with a corresponding

body of priests, to which the ruler most certainly belonged."

WARFARE AND THE ORIGIN OF THE STATE

Contemporary theories on the origin of the state, such as that of Carneiro (1970), often give a decisive role to warfare:

> "...there is little question that, in one way or another, war played a decisive role in the rise of the state. Historical or archeological evidence of war is found in the early stages of state formation in Mesopotamia, Egypt, India, China, Japan, Greece, Rome, northern Europe, central Africa, Polynesia, Middle America, Peru, and Colombia, to name only the most prominent examples."

Carneiro's analysis of the early state corresponds to the descriptions that we have seen above, involving military leadership and a class-structured society based on slaves that were taken prisoner through warfare:

> "While the aggregation of villages into chiefdoms, and of chiefdoms into kingdoms, was occurring by external acquisition, the structure of these increasingly larger political units was being elaborated by internal evolution. These inner changes were, of course, closely related to outer events. The expansion of successful states brought within their borders conquered peoples and territory which had to be administered. And it was the individuals who had distinguished themselves in war who were generally appointed to political office and assigned the task of carrying out this

administration. Besides maintaining law and order and collecting taxes, the functions of this burgeoning class of administrators included mobilizing labor for building irrigation works, roads, fortresses, palaces, and temples. Thus, their functions helped to weld an assorted collection of petty states into a single integrated and centralized political unit.

These same individuals, who owed their improved social position to their exploits in war, became, along with the ruler and his kinsmen, the nucleus of an upper class. A lower class in turn emerged from the prisoners taken in war and employed as servants and slaves by their captors. In this manner did war contribute to the rise of social classes"

The Carneiro thesis on war and the state was not new, although he added an aspect concerning the importance of geographical barriers so those defeated in battle could not escape and were therefore subjugated. For example, prior to reviewing Carneiro's theory, Otterbein (1973) mentions many earlier approaches that also considered warfare as crucial to the origin of the state:

> "Spencer (1896), an evolutionist, argues that leadership and subordination developed first in the military and were then transferred to the political system. Thus an increase in the efficiency of the military resulted in an increase in political centralization. The "conquest theory of the state" is developed by Gumplowicz (1899: 119): "states have never arisen except through the subjection of one stock by another, or by several others in alliance ... No state has arisen without original ethnical heterogeneity ..."

> Conquest theory is further developed by Oppenheimer (1914: 55-81)..."

The Carneiro analysis is not universally accepted, and there are other theories that do not give such a central place to warfare. For example, in his books *The Early State* (1978) and *Development and Decline: The Evolution of Sociopolitical Organization* (1985), H. J. M. Claessen downplays the importance of warfare, although as Carneiro (1987) points out in his review, other authors in the latter book acknowledge it:

> "Since Claessen minimizes, if he does not actually deny, the effect of war and population pressure on the rise of the state, it is not surprising that he should reject the circumscription theory of state formation, which relies heavily on both (p. 257). But if Claessen gives the circumscription theory short shrift, some contributors to the volume appear more sympathetic. Bargatsky, for instance, writes that "In Hawaii, Tahiti, and Tonga a development along the lines indicated by Carneiro (1970) was well under way in precontact times" (p. 309). Even stronger support comes from Ronald Cohen, who says, "In effect, warfare . . . plus circumscription, produces statehood. States not only make war, but war makes states" (p. 279; see also p. 278)."

Some more recent studies such as that of the formation of the Zulu state in the 19th Century, tend to confirm the Carneiro analysis. Mathieu Deflem (1999), in his article, *Warfare, Political Leadership, and State Formation: The case of the Zulu Kingdom, 1808-1879*, says that "Carneiro's theory explains the origin and territorial expansion of the Zulu Empire." Deflem also gives credit to the theory of Elwood Service concerning the transition from chiefdoms to the bona fide state, and in this case the very definition of the state is related to warfare and its monopoly on the use of force.:

> "The crucial characteristic of political states is that central authority becomes fully established and institutionalized in formally regulated offices. State-controlled laws are formal, and judicial offices are assigned to act as third parties. Unlike chiefdoms, the political structure of states is fully differentiated, visible and territorially bounded. States have a monopoly over the threat or use of physical force, both internally, through a formalized judicial and punitive system of repressive laws, and externally, by means of an organized and permanent army."

The very definition of the state for sociologists like Max Weber depends on warfare and the monopoly of force. Weber (1921) defined the state as the organization that has a "monopoly on the legitimate use of physical force within a given territory." As mentioned above, the Harappan civilization has been considered "stateless" precisely because it did not have warfare. In describing that civilization Thompson defines the state as "an organization exercising 'paramount control' over society (Fried 1967, 237), that is, monopolizing all *large-scale* use of force - and often acquiring routine acceptance of its 'legitimacy' (as emphasized by Weber)."

Why was the Harappan civilization unusual in not developing warfare or a state organization. Thompson speculates that the agricultural and commercial basis for the development of its cities was so dispersed that warfare would not have been "profitable":

It can be argued that the Harappan example supports the Carneiro thesis that warfare plays a decisive role of warfare in the origin of the state; because the Harappan people did not engage very much in war, they never developed a state, and certainly not an empire in the classic sense. At the same time, however, it also provides an example in addition that of Crete, of an ancient civilization that was not engaged in extensive warfare. As so often in scientific analysis, it is the exception that proves the rule.

RELIGION AND THE ORIGIN OF THE STATE

The account of the origin of the state by Leslie A. White (1959) in *The Evolution of Culture*, considers that the state and the church were one and the same at the time that the state emerged. White provides abundant historical examples:

> "Originally, i.e., with the advent of civil society, the church and the state were one, as Herbert Spencer astutely observed many years ago [1896].
>
> "...In ancient Peru, the head of the state and the head of the church were brothers, or uncle and nephew; and the former was a god, or descended from the sun god. In Egypt, the pharaoh was for ages god, priest, and king, at least in theory. In practice, the pharaoh had of necessity to delegate the worship of the gods to priests, who acquired thereby so much autonomy as virtually

to constitute a church structurally distinct from the state.

In the early urban cultures of Mesopotamia, 'priestly and secular functions no doubt rested in one and the same person.' [Jastrow, 1915] In ancient Sumer, 'church and state were so bound together that those exercising authority formed a theocracy, functioning on the one hand religiously and on the other secularly.' (Turner 1941] The kings of Assyria were priests originally, and they 'retain their priestly functions through all periods of the kingdom.' [Jastrow, 1915] 'Church and State are one in India.' [Hocart, 1950]. In Greece during the Iron Age the king was also a priest. Many pagan ruling families of Scandinavia reckoned their descent from Nordic deities, even as the modern Japanese trace their Emperor to divine ancestry. Caesar was Pontifex maximus as well as emperor in imperial Rome; Augustus likewise served as the head of the state religion."

The church was responsible for providing legitimacy to the state and for keeping the citizenry in line by using theology and ritual to install obedience, docility and loyalty to the state. As described by White:

"The military force of the state was not enough to cope with the chronic and ever-recurring threat of insurrection, civil war, and anarchy; the resources of the church must be employed to this end also. So it was that the priests taught the masses, and validated these teachings with the wonders and mysteries of religion, that they should accept, and even defend the established order. For the Egyptians, the universe was a moral order established by the sun god, Re, and their social ideal involved 'a full acceptance of class status, the inferiority of labor, and poverty as the ordinary condition of common men; these, indeed, were aspects of the divine moral order.' [Turner, 1941]. Buddhism taught men and women to be content with their lot and station in life. The teaching of Confucius 'devoted its whole attention to making people recognize their betters with distinction,' according to Ku Chieh-kang, 'and that is certainly a most advantageous theory to an autocratic despot.' More recently, the Roman Catholic Church has recognized the utility and function of religion as means of preventing insurrection by 'subduing the souls of men:'"

White provides the following excerpt from the Encyclical of Pope Benedict XV, explaining that the role of religion is to "subdue the souls of men":

"Only too well does experience show that when religion is banished, human authority totters to its fall... when the rulers of the people disdain the authority of God, the people in turn despise the authority of men. There remains, it is true the usual expedient of suppressing rebellion by force; but to what effect? Force subdues the bodies of men, not their souls."

The relation of religions to the state is very contradictory when seen in historical perspective. While state religions were being used to support the state's culture of war, other religions arose in opposition to the state's culture of war. Their prophets spoke of non-violence and brotherhood instead of violence and enemy images, and they gave rise to the great religions of later history. In the period around 800-400 BC, called the "Axial Age" by the philosopher Karl Jaspers (1953), Confucius taught in China, the Siddhartha Gautama (Buddha) taught in India, Zoroastrianism arose in Persia and Jainism in India, the Upanishads were written in India, Elijah, Isaiah and Jeremiah prophesied in Israel, foreshadowing the life and teachings of Jesus and Mohammad at a later time.

. Once again, however, over the course of history, the major religions that had arisen in opposition to the state were, in many cases, co-opted by the state to provide legitimacy to state power and to keep the people in line. As a result, the major religions are complex, containing at the same time both a "peaceable garden culture" as well as a "holy war culture." in the words of Elise Boulding (2000).

A SUMMARY OF THE CULTURE OF WAR AT THE DAWN OF HISTORY

The preceding descriptions, with the exceptions of Crete and Harappan civilizations, provide a clear picture of warfare at the dawn of history. The usefulness of war was completely transformed by the state from its usefulness in prehistory:

> 1. A source of wealth in terms of plunder and slavery
> 2. A means of defense against attacks by other states
> 3. A means of internal control to deter or defeat internal revolt

The scope of the culture of war associated with warfare was expanded, but included all six of the aspects that had evolved during history, plus five others. The first eight of its aspects below correspond to those listed in the original UNESCO document on the culture of peace (United Nations 1998), while the last three are added here:

1. armies and armaments
2. authoritarian rule associated with military leadership
3. control of information through secrecy and propaganda
4. identification of an "enemy"
5. education of young men from the nobility to be warriors
6. male domination
7. wealth based on plunder and slavery
8. economy based on exploitation of people (slaves, serfs, etc.) and the environment
9. religious institutions that support the government and military
10. artistic and literary glorification of military conquest
11. means to deter slave revolts and political dissidents including internal use of military power, prisons, penal systems and executions.

All of the various aspects of the culture of war at the dawn of history were inter-related, forming a single integrated system in which each aspect reinforces the others. This corresponds to the description of cultural phenomena by Leslie A. White (1959) that was quoted in the first section of the present book. The causal relationship between warfare and the culture of war is in both directions: warfare produces a culture of war and a culture of war produces war.

One important aspect of the culture of war in the above list did not receive very much attention in the accounts that we have quoted and needs further discussion in the following section:

> 11. means to deter slave revolts and political dissidents including internal use of military power, prisons, penal systems and executions.

THE INTERNAL CULTURE OF WAR: A TABOO TOPIC

It is not easy to document the history of the internal use of military power to deter and suppress internal revolts, or the prisons and executions associated with it. It is hardly mentioned in the UNESCO history. However, we may assume that the internal use of military power has been one of the important functions of the culture of war since the beginning of civilization, as described by Leslie A. White (1959) in *The Evolution of Culture*:

> "Warfare tends to maintain and even to intensify the class structure of nations. Peoples of the vanquished nation are subjugated. The masses of the victorious nation have become subordinated to absolute rule as a condition of waging war, while the ruling class becomes enriched and more strongly entrenched in power.
>
> "*Class struggles:* The lot of the subordinate class is often a hard one, and excessive privation and toil, coupled frequently with harsh and brutal treatment, incite them to revolt. Slave revolts, insurrections of serfs, uprisings of

peasants are chronic and periodic occurrences in civil society.

An insurrection of the masses took place in Egypt as early as 2200 B.C., according to Moret and Turner. Another uprising occurred during the Twentieth Dynasty. 'Both had their origin in the failure of the ruling classes to permit the masses to have sufficient food,' says Turner, 'and both were accompanied by disorder, murder, and robbery.' Iranian peasants rose against the priests and nobles in the Mazdakian revolt about A.D. 500, seizing land and cattle and transforming their villages into communistic communities. There were uprisings of peasants and miners in China under the early Han emperors. In Sparta, secret agents circulated among the *helots,* one of the two servile classes, to search out and kill 'anyone who was disobedient or showed signs of possessing superior intelligence.' A quarter of a million slaves rose in revolt in Sicily in the second century B.C. They were starved into submission, and thousands of them were crucified. A slave revolt in Italy led by Spartacus in 73 B.C. was eventually put down on the field of battle; 6,000 of his followers were crucified along the Appian Way. These are but a few examples of the countless insurrections and uprisings throughout the length and breadth of civil society for centuries on end."

It is the business of the state ... to put down these insurrections in order to preserve the integrity of the nation within which they occur.

And the sternest measures are employed in this process..."

In modern times we have interior ministries, police forces, national guard forces, and a range of prisons and other punitive institutions to maintain internal control, but it is not clear from the descriptions of early empires how revolts by political dissidents and slaves were normally kept in check. We may assume that military force, imprisonment and execution were employed. We know, of course, that Socrates was imprisoned and executed by the Greeks and Jesus by the Romans, and there are stories like the following about the control of slaves, this story coming from ancient Rome (Bennetts 2002) :

> "In 61 AD, Nero's urban prefect was murdered by one of his slaves. Under an earlier Augustan law, every slave under the same roof at the time of such a murder was to be put to death as a deterrent. The entire household of 400 slaves, including men women and children were condemned to death, despite the protests of some members of the Roman Senate against the punishment of women, children and the innocent."

One historian who dealt with this question was Friedrich Engels, concerned, along with his close collaborator Karl Marx, with the question of class struggle. In his book *Origin of the Family, Private Property and the State*, Engels (1884) makes the point that the state, from its very beginning, required a "special public force" to maintain its class structure.

> "The second distinguishing characteristic [of the state] is the institution of a public force which is

no longer immediately identical with the people's own organization of themselves as an armed power. This special public force is needed because a self-acting armed organization of the people has become impossible since their cleavage into classes. The slaves also belong to the population: as against the 365,000 slaves, the 90,000 Athenian citizens constitute only a privileged class. The people's army of the Athenian democracy confronted the slaves as an aristocratic public force, and kept them in check; but to keep the citizens in check as well, a police-force was needed, as described above. This public force exists in every state; it consists not merely of armed men, but also of material appendages, prisons and coercive institutions of all kinds."

The lack of attention to the internal function of war is all the more remarkable since the internal use of force is essential to the very definition of the state. In general, it receives so little attention in the descriptions of ancient civilizations (both by those civilizations at the time and by contemporary historians), that we may consider it as a taboo topic. The taboo against its discussion continues to the present day, as will be considered in the following section.

What is the origin of this taboo?

Early empires, as described above, glorified their *external* military exploits against foreign enemies in their propaganda, art and religion, while they downplayed the *internal* use of the military to maintain order within the state. The glorification of the power of violence of the military rulers against external enemies should have impressed the citizenry sufficiently to discourage revolt. If, on the other hand, the rulers had emphasized the internal use of the military, it might have been counter-productive, producing a climate of fear and suspicion, much as Thucydides described when Hellenic society "became divided into camps in which no man trusted his fellow." As described above by White, religious institutions played an important role in supporting the internal culture of war by masking its force with elaborate rituals and teachings. The ruler was not said to rule by force but by religious "divine right." Over time, the capacity of the state for internal intervention became assumed but not questioned. Those who dared to raise questions would risk being considered as subversive.

THE EVOLUTION OF THE CULTURE OF WAR OVER THE PAST 5,000 YEARS: ITS INCREASING MONOPOLIZATION BY THE STATE

During the 5,000 years from the beginning of recorded history to the present time the culture of war has become more and more monopolized by the state, retaining the three functions: conquest, defense and internal control (the latter remaining a taboo topic). The involvement of the state with the culture of war has become stronger over the course of history as the state has prevented the development of warfare by other social structures and it has enlisted new partners, including capitalist business and industry during recent centuries. Although warfare has frequently occurred outside of state structures, with one set of exceptions, stateless warfare has not been dominant. The most important exceptions were from the 4th to 13th Centuries after the fall of the Roman empire when much of the world was overrun by nomadic warring tribes originating in Central Asia, the Xiongnu and the Huns followed by the Turks and the Mongols (see the UNESCO History of Humanity, Volume III). It is a tribute to the modern assumption of the dominance of the state that this period is often called the "Dark Ages."

Over the course of time the economic benefits of plunder and slavery have been extended and replaced by colonialism and neo-colonialism externally and by feudalism and then capitalist exploitation internally. In reaction to these developments, a fourth function of war has appeared: revolution and national liberation by which the ruling class of the previous state may be replaced by a new ruling class with its own culture of war that had been refined through the revolutionary process. Two increasingly important aspects of the culture of war in recent years have been the military-industrial complex and the international "drugs-for-guns" trade. The culture that supports war has been further reinforced by the invention and use of racism and nationalism.

The greatest change in the culture of war has been the enormous expansion of control of information including control of the mass media, overtly or covertly, by state power and its allies in the military-industrial complex. Other than these changes, however, the fundamental nature of the culture of war has remained remarkably stable since the beginning of recorded history: it has become increasingly a monopoly of the state, essential to the maintenance of state power.

Before considering the state in detail, we need to consider claims that two other institutions, the multi-national corporation and the United Nations, have taken over functions of war and the culture of war traditionally carried out by the state.

It has become fashionable in certain academic and political circles to say that the role of the state as the decisive power in the world is being taken over by the multi-national corporation. Sometimes it is said that the multi-national corporation has now taken control of neo-colonialism or imperialism.

There is an extensive literature on the influence of the multi-national corporation on state policy, including its influence on the political decisions concerning the culture of war. At this point, however, let us ask a more restricted question, "Have the multi-national corporations taken on a decisive role in the culture of war?" To answer this question, let us consider armies, armaments and armed conflict. Although many multi-national corporations have their own internal police forces, sometimes armed with heavy arms such as helicopters and machine guns, in no case do they have the same power as the military forces of even rather small states. Also, in some cases they engage mercenary forces, such as, for example, those have been engaged to guard oil facilities in Iraq and Colombia. In a few cases they have been involved directly in the overthrow of legitimate states, for example the role of International Telephone and Telegraph in the overthrow of the Chilean government of Allende. In that case, however, they did not act on their own, but in concert with the CIA and the secret approval of the U.S. government. Similarly, in Nigeria, the Rivers State Internal Security Force, though it is funded by the Shell Oil Company to protect their installations, is still officially a military branch of the government.

To summarize, at the present time there is little evidence from actual armed conflict or material preparation for armed conflict that the multi-nationals have usurped the role of the state as the major player in the culture of war.

In fact, the state's internal culture of war ensures that it retains a monopoly on the use of force within its territory. If a multi-national corporation were to begin establishing a private army within the boundaries of an established state, one could imagine that the state would force it to disband or limit it. There are two exceptions. One is the case of paramilitary forces that are, in fact, secretly related to state power (for example, today in Colombia). The other exceptions are revolutionary movements that try to conceal their development of armed forces or else take advantage of mountainous terrain such as Fidel Castro and Che Guevara did in Cuba, or as is now taking place with the Taleban and its allies in the mountains between Afghanistan and Pakistan.

In two particular aspects of the culture of war the multi-nationals have become major players: the use of the mass media for propaganda and the production of armaments by the military-industrial complex. These will be discussed further below, but in both cases, these functions are carried out in coordination with and not independent of the state.

The United Nations, in the eyes of some observers, was designed to become a superior authority in the world that would replace the power of the state. If this were to occur, then the UN could, in theory, assume or replace the role of the state as the major actor in the culture of war. However, this has not come to pass.

From the inception of the United Nations until the 1990s, after the fall of the Soviet Empire, the United Nations was prevented by the Cold War from expanding its powers, as the East and West could not agree on policies in the Security Council. After the fall of the Soviet Empire, the UN Security Council was able to act by consensus. The Council endorsed the attack on Iraq in the first war of the Persian Gulf, and there seemed to be some movement towards the UN as a super-power. When I was working in the UN system I was told that the 38th floor of the UN Secretariat building in New York had become like a military headquarters with uniformed military men from the U.S. and NATO saluting each other as they passed in the corridor. That was the when the Secretary-General issued his proposal entitled *An Agenda for Peace* (United Nations 1992).

A close analysis of *An Agenda for Peace* suggests that it would have been more appropriately named, *An Agenda for War by the United Nations.* The concept of "peace" was the old concept meaning the "absence of war" and the document did not address the culture of war. Instead, it proposed that the United Nations establish a standing military force that would be ready to intervene at the discretion of the Security Council. In practical terms, that means at the discretion of the five super-powers who control the Security Council: France, UK, US, Russia and China.

The proposal for a standing UN military force has not been implemented, and I am not aware of anyone who seriously believes that it will ever be implemented. It may be assumed, for want of a better explanation, that the Member States of the United Nations simply have no desire to cede their military authority to any other body. There are some regional military agreements, such as NATO in Europe, but even in the case of NATO there is often a tension between the demands on the combined force and reluctance by European states to contribute further. For example, as of this writing, France has not rejoined the integrated military command of NATO from which it withdrew under DeGaulle in 1966.

In fact, the states show no serious intention of giving their war-making power to the United Nations. Instead, the state remains the principle agent of the culture of war.

The very definition of the state for sociologists like Max Weber depends on warfare and the monopoly of force. As mentioned earlier, his definition of the state is the organization that has a "monopoly on the legitimate use of physical force within a given territory" (Weber 1921).

The definition of the "failed state" similarly depends on the monopoly of force, in this case, a failed state is one that has lost the monopoly of force. Although the UN has not undertaken a precise definition of this term, in practice it coincides with the following definition to be found in Wikipedia:

> "A state could be said to 'succeed' if it maintains a monopoly on the legitimate use of physical force within its borders. When this is broken (e.g., through the dominant presence of warlords, militias, or terrorism), the very existence of the state becomes dubious, and the state becomes a *failed state*."

The definition of the state as the "organization that has a monopoly on the legitimate use of physical force within a given territory" has remained valid from the origin of the state until the present time. This monopolization has ensured that the state has no competition from other potential sources of war or a culture of war. In *The Evolution of Culture*, Leslie A. White (1959) traces throughout history how the state has monopolized "an exclusive right to kill." This, he says, indicates "the achievement of full status of civil society."

> "With the advent of civil society private vengeance becomes outlawed, and the state assumes an exclusive right to kill. This applies

both to personal vengeance and private 'wars,' such as used to be fought by Scottish clans. Blood revenge had been outlawed in ancient Aztec and Inca states, and in Negro monarchies such as those of the Ganda and the Dahomeans. The state had exclusive jurisdiction over crimes in ancient Egypt and Mesopotamia. The outlawing of private vengeance and wars is one of the best indications that could be cited of the achievement of full status of civil society. It is interesting to note, however that this point was reached rather late among Germanic peoples and in England. 'As late as 1439,' according to Munroe Smith, the schöffen (criminal judges) of Namur declared in a judgment: 'If the kin of the slain man will and can avenge him, good luck to them, for with this matter we schöffen have nothing to do.' And as recently as the fifteenth century in England, a private war was fought between two noblemen and their followers [Tylor 1881]."

As we will see in the following pages, the state's monopoly on violence has increased in strength and complexity over the course of history, and evidence suggests that this trend is continuing. Although revolutionary wars and wars of national liberation break the monopoly of force of the previous state, they do not break the cycle of state violence. Instead, the revolutionaries establish a new state with a new monopoly on violence.

In sum, the eleven aspects listed previously for the culture of war at the dawn of civilization has been expanded to at least fifteen, with the addition of the military-industrial complex, the drug-for-guns trade, nationalism and racism:

1. armies and armaments
2. neocolonialism
3. the internal culture of war and economies based on exploitation (capitalist exploitation of workers, as well as exploitation and destruction of the environment)
4. prisons and penal systems
5. the military-industrial complex
6. the drugs-for-guns trade
7. authoritarian rule associated with military leadership
8. control of information through secrecy and propaganda
9. identification of an "enemy"
10. education for a culture of war
11. male domination
12. religious institutions that support the government and military
13. artistic and literary glorification of military conquest
14. nationalism
15. racism, both institutional and attitudinal

Let's now look at these 15 aspects in some detail.

1. Armies and armaments

One could write an entire book just about the cultural identity of the warrior over the course of recorded history. Suffice it to say, without going into detail, that the culture of the individual warrior has become more and more complex and unique along with the evolution of the state and the increased hierarchy and specialization of armies and complexity of armaments.

Despite predictions that that the buildup of armies and armaments would decrease after the end of the Cold War, they have returned to the highest levels in history. Nuclear arms and their continued proliferation have added an especially dangerous dimension with their potential to destroy all life on the planet.

The priority devoted by the state to the culture of war can be measured to some extent by the proportion of its budget dedicated to military spending.. Here is a summary of national military expenditures for 1999 as published by the United States Department of State (2001). which seems to be the most recent data available on military spending as a percentage of central government expenditures. These figures range from 4.2 to 22.4 percent. They are probably underestimates; for example, according to the Friends Committee on National Legislation (2008), the U.S. government in 2006 devoted 28% of its budget to current military spending and another 13% to debt payment for past military spending, a total of 41%. This is much greater than the 15.7% admitted in the official government figures. Much of the difference also comes from U.S. government insistence on including social security entitlements as part of central government expenditures, even though it is simply reimbursing the investments that have been made by the citizen payments.

> All states: 10.1%
> Selected states:
> Russia 22.4%
> China 22.2%
> United States: 15.7%
> United Kingdom 6.9%
> France 5.9% (estimated)

Regions:
Middle East 21.4%
South Asia 16.1%
North America 14.6%
Africa 14.0%
East Asia 12.7%
Central Asia and Caucasus 9.2%
South America 7.6%
Oceania 7.0%
Europe 6.3%
Central America 4.2%

As mentioned earlier, it is the external functions of war and the culture of war that have been given the most attention, while as we will see later, the internal functions have remained, for the most part, a taboo topic.

Two external functions may be distinguished, although in practice they are closely related. One is the function of war and the culture of war for defense against external attack, and the other is the function for external conquest and exploitation. Today, most states tend to emphasize the former. For example, they speak of the "Ministry of Defense" rather than the "Ministry of External Conquest" or, as in past times, the "Ministry of Colonial Rule". Under the present conditions of neo-colonialism, the major military powers speak of defending their "national interest," even though it is done through military bases and interventions in places far away from the home country.

2. *External conquest and exploitation: colonialism and neo-colonialism*

Looking back over history, it is clear that conquest and exploitation have remained a major function of warfare between nations, although its nature has changed. In the centuries leading up to the 20th Century, it consisted mainly of European colonialism. Although the Europeans considered themselves to be at peace, as far as the colonized peoples were concerned colonialism was a form of conquest and war. Lenin (1917) described this in especially blunt terms during the First World War in *War and Revolution*. What Lenin describes is our distinction between war and the underlying culture of war which he calls as "the entire system of European states in their economic and political interrelations":

> "Peace reigned in Europe, but this was because domination over hundreds of millions of people in the colonies by the European nations was sustained only through constant, incessant, interminable wars, which we Europeans do not regard as wars at all, since all too often they resembled, not wars, but brutal massacres, the wholesale slaughter of unarmed peoples. The thing is that if we want to know what the present war is about we must first of all make a general survey of the policies of the European powers as a whole. We must not take this or that example, this or that particular case, which can easily be wrenched out of the context of social phenomena and which is worthless, because an opposite example can just as easily be cited. We must take the whole policy of the entire system of European states in their economic and political interrelations if we are to understand how the present war steadily and inevitably grew out of this system."

Colonialism brought racism, a new and especially vicious aspect of the culture of war. A particularly vivid account of this process was made by the Algerian revolutionary and psychologist, Franz Fanon, in his 1959 book *Wretched of the Earth*, a book that had considerable influence among those fighting for national liberation:

> "Colonial domination, because it is total and tends to over-simplify, very soon manages to disrupt in spectacular fashion the cultural life of a conquered people. This cultural obliteration is made possible by the negation of national reality, by new legal relations introduced by the occupying power, by the banishment of the natives and their customs to outlying districts by colonial society, by expropriation, and by the systematic enslaving of men and women. ... Every effort is made to bring the colonised person to admit the inferiority of his culture which has been transformed into instinctive patterns of behaviour, to recognise the unreality of his 'nation', and, in the last extreme, the confused and imperfect character of his own biological structure."

As national liberation movements gained ground in the middle of the 20th Century, colonialism could not be sustained, and it was replaced by neo-colonialism. A classic first-hand description of neo-colonialism is provided by Kwame Nkrumah, President of the first newly-liberated African nation, Ghana, in his book *Neo-Colonialism, the Last Stage of Imperialism* (1965). Now, over 40 years later, with the exception of a few named personalities, Nkrumah's analysis holds true as much as ever:

> "Faced with the militant peoples of the ex-colonial territories in Asia, Africa, the Caribbean and Latin America, imperialism simply switches tactics.

Without a qualm it dispenses with its flags, and even with certain of its more hated expatriate officials. This means, so it claims, that it is 'giving' independence to its former subjects, to be followed by 'aid' for their development. Under cover of such phrases, however, it devises innumerable ways to accomplish objectives formerly achieved by naked colonialism. It is this sum total of these modern attempts to perpetuate colonialism while at the same time talking about 'freedom', which has come to be known as *neo-colonialism*.

Foremost among the neo-colonialists is the United States, which has long exercised its power in Latin America. Fumblingly at first she turned towards Europe, and then with more certainty after world war two when most countries of that continent were indebted to her. Since then, with methodical thoroughness and touching attention to detail, the Pentagon set about consolidating its ascendancy, evidence of which can be seen all around the world.

Who really rules in such places as Great Britain, West Germany, Japan, Spain, Portugal or Italy? If General de Gaulle is 'defecting' from U.S. monopoly control, what interpretation can be placed on his 'experiments' in the Sahara desert, his paratroopers in Gabon, or his trips to Cambodia and Latin America?

Lurking behind such questions are the extended tentacles of the Wall Street octopus. And its suction cups and muscular strength are provided by a phenomenon dubbed 'The Invisible Government', arising from Wall Street's connection with the Pentagon and various intelligence services ..."

"Still another neo-colonialist trap on the economic front has come to be known as 'multilateral aid' through international organisations: the International Monetary Fund, the International Bank for Reconstruction and Development (known as the World Bank), the International Finance Corporation and the International Development Association are examples, all, significantly, having U.S. capital as their major backing. These agencies have the habit of forcing would-be borrowers to submit to various offensive conditions, such as supplying information about their economies, submitting their policy and plans to review by the World Bank and accepting agency supervision of their use of loans ..."

"Nor is the whole story of 'aid' contained in figures, for there are conditions which hedge it around: the conclusion of commerce and navigation treaties; agreements for economic co-operation; the right to meddle in internal finances, including currency and foreign exchange, to lower trade barriers in favour of the donor country's goods and capital; to protect the interests of private investments; determination of how the funds are to be used; forcing the recipient to set up counterpart funds; to supply raw materials to the donor; and use of such funds a majority of it, in fact to buy goods from the donor nation. These conditions apply to industry, commerce, agriculture, shipping and insurance, apart from others which are political and military."

Nkrumah goes on to describe the full culture of neo-colonialism, including not only economic, but also cultural manipulation including by means of the arts, the mass media and religion. Once again we see that the culture of war extends far deeper than war alone:

> "In the labour field, for example, imperialism operates through labour arms like the Social Democratic parties of Europe led by the British Labour Party, and through such instruments as the International Confederation of Free Trade Unions (ICFTU), now apparently being superseded by the New York Africa-American Labour Centre (AALC) under AFL-CIO chief George Meany and the well-known CIA man in labour's top echelons, Irving Brown ..."

> "Even the cinema stories of fabulous Hollywood are loaded. One has only to listen to the cheers of an African audience as Hollywood's heroes slaughter red Indians or Asiatics to understand the effectiveness of this weapon. For, in the developing continents, where the colonialist heritage has left a vast majority still illiterate, even the smallest child gets the message contained in the blood and thunder stories emanating from California. And along with murder and the Wild West goes an incessant barrage of anti-socialist propaganda, in which the trade union man, the revolutionary, or the man of dark skin is generally cast as the villain, while the policeman, the gum-shoe, the Federal agent - in a word, the CIA - type spy is ever the hero. Here, truly, is the ideological under-belly of those political murders which so often use local people as their instruments.

While Hollywood takes care of fiction, the enormous monopoly press, together with the outflow of slick, clever, expensive magazines, attends to what it chooses to call 'news.' Within separate countries, one or two news agencies control the news handouts, so that a deadly uniformity is achieved, regardless of the number of separate newspapers or magazines; while internationally, the financial preponderance of the United States is felt more and more through its foreign correspondents and offices abroad, as well as through its influence over inter-national capitalist journalism. Under this guise, a flood of anti-liberation propaganda emanates from the capital cities of the West, directed against China, Vietnam, Indonesia, Algeria, Ghana and all countries which hack out their own independent path to freedom. Prejudice is rife. For example, wherever there is armed struggle against the forces of reaction, the nationalists are referred to as rebels, terrorists, or frequently 'communist terrorists'!

Perhaps one of the most insidious methods of the neo-colonialists is evangelism. Following the liberation movement there has been a veritable riptide of religious sects, the overwhelming majority of them American. Typical of these are Jehovah's Witnesses who recently created trouble in certain developing countries by busily teaching their citizens not to salute the new national flags. Religion was too thin to smother the outcry that arose against this activity, and a temporary lull followed. But the number of evangelists continues to grow."

As Nkrumah correctly emphasizes, the countries of the North have engaged the United Nations as a partner in their neo-colonialist exploitation of the South. Although the International Monetary Fund and the World Bank claim to benefit the poor countries of the South, in effect they manipulate and pressure their economies so as to make them better targets for investment and profit-making by the multinational corporations based in the North. This is described in the following excerpt from a editorial in the Ecologist (2000) :

> "One of the World Bank's central roles is to ensure developing countries have the physical infrastructure necessary to facilitate their integration into the global economy so as to enable the exploitation of their resources, cheap labour, and consumers by Northern corporations. To that end, it provides loans for the construction of roads, ports, mines, hydroelectric dams, oil wells and pipelines, and coal-fired power stations, mostly built, once again, by Northern corporations -- who received nearly $5 billion in direct loans and guarantees for this purpose from the Bank's private sector arms last year alone. Revenues generated rarely reach the poor. Instead, the poor are often displaced from their homes, suffer loss or damage to their natural resource base, and are placed in the front line of climatic destabilisation that the Bank's support for fossil fuels is helping to cause.
>
> The World Bank and the IMF also provide loans (totalling $18 billion from the Bank alone last year) to debt-ridden or near-bankrupt developing countries in exchange for the introduction of structural adjustment reforms that remove all

constraints on Northern corporations seeking to export/import raw materials, and invest or locate there. The predicament of these countries is exploited to exert enormous control over their governments which is used to ensure the bulk of public expenditure and economic activity is channelled into debt repayments to Northern banks and investors. In the process, once again, the poor are hit the hardest, as jobs are cut, health and education budgets slashed, price supports removed, and food and natural resources exported abroad."

The continued support of neo-colonialism by the World Bank and International Monetary Fund are assured by its voting structure. It is a club of the rich, with votes allotted in proportion to financial contributions, and the United States in charge. There is no pretense of democracy here.

3. The internal culture of war and economies based on exploitation of workers and of the environment

If there is one overall trend that has been steady and certain over recent centuries it is the increasing gap between the rich and the poor, both within and between countries. No matter what language you wish to use, whether it be the language of Marx and Engels in the Communist Manifesto, or the theories of Nobel Prize winning economists from the heart of the capitalist class, it is clear that this is the result of exploitation of workers by capitalists. Over time the state has always played a central role; in the words of Engels (1884): "The ancient state was, above all, the state of the slave-owners for holding down the slaves, just as the feudal state was the organ of the nobility for holding down the peasant serfs and bondsmen, and the modern representative state is the instrument for exploiting wage-labor by capital." At each stage of this history, exploitation has been enforced by the internal culture of war.

During the first centuries of the American colonies and the new republic of the United States, internal intervention was used to prevent slaves from rebelling in the South This is described in my 1995 article in the Journal of Peace Research, *Internal Military Interventions in the United States*:

> "The South was an armed camp for the purpose of enforcing slavery prior to the Civil War. In his survey of American Negro slave revolts, Aptheker (1943) found records of about 250 revolts and conspiracies, but said that this was no doubt an underestimate. Most of the revolts were suppressed by state militia, for which records are not readily available. In addition to suppressing revolts, the military enforced a state of martial law. According to Mahon (1983) in his *History of the Militia and the National Guard*, before the U.S. Revolution, 'the primary mission of the slave states' militia increasingly became the slave patrol' (p. 22) and after the revolution, 'the slave states continued to require militiamen to do patrol duty to discourage slave insurrections' (p. 54).
>
> The militarization of Southern cities was described by F. L. Olmstead in the late 1850s, as quoted by Aptheker (1943, p. 69):
>
> '...police machinery such as you never find in towns under free government: citadels, sentries, passports, grapeshotted cannon, and daily public

> whippings. ...more than half of the inhabitants of this town were subject to arrest, imprisonment and barbarous punishment if found in the streets without a passport after the evening 'gunfire'. Similar precautions and similar customs may be discovered in every large town in the South. ...a military - organization which is invested with more arbitrary and cruel power than any police in Europe.'"

Although slavery was abolished in most countries by the end of the 19th Century, its place was taken by the exploitation of industrial and agricultural wage workers. At this point the internal culture of war was transformed to prevent and suppress workers' strikes, revolts and revolutions, as described in my article on internal military interventions:

> "The strike wave of 1877 transformed internal military intervention in the USA into industrial warfare. It began with a railroad strike in West Virginia, which spread throughout the industrial states. Before it was over, 45,000 militia had been called into action, along with 2,000 federal troops on active duty and practically the entire U.S. Army on alert (Riker, 1957, pp. 47-48). To realize the scope of this mobilization, one needs to know that according to Riker there were only 47,000 militia used during the entire Civil War, and the size of the entire U.S. Army around 1877 was 25,000 (p. 41). From 1877 to 1900, the U.S. Army was used extensively in labor disputes and a shared interest developed between the officer corps and U.S. industrialists (Cooper, 1980).

The 1877 intervention gave birth to the modern National Guard. This point is agreed upon by the principal histories of the Guard (Derthick, 1965; Mahon, 1983; and Riker, 1957). As Riker documents in detail, not only did all of the states establish their National Guard at that time, but also the appropriations of the new Guard were almost perfectly correlated with the number of strikers in that state. He concludes that 'in short it is reasonable to infer that the primary motive for the revival of the militia was a felt need for an industrial police' (p. 55)."

In recent years there has been a convergence of neo-colonialism and the capitalist exploitation of industrial and agricultural wage workers. Industrial enterprises in the North have largely re-located into countries of the South, decreasing the industrial class struggle within the North and re-locating it to the South.

The use of the military for internal control has changed but not diminished in recent centuries. As mentioned above it has been used especially in the United States (and presumably other capitalist countries although data are not available) for the control of industrial workers. It has also been used for the prevention and suppression of revolutionary movements; for example, the development and frequent deployment of the CRS in France, an internal military force developed after the student rebellion of 1968 which threatened at the time to be joined by a workers' revolution as well. On the other side, newly established revolutionary governments also used the military to prevent counter-revolution, and to establish a chain of command throughout the country to replace previous mechanism of capitalism or feudalism. In the newly revolutionary China, the power base of the Communist Party and the government has been the Red Army. In the early days of the Soviet Union, Trotsky proposed that industrial production be organized primarily on the basis of military forced labor camps, and later Stalin brought this to pass. Ironically, when the Soviet Empire finally crashed in 1989 the military stayed in its barracks and did not intervene.

In the United States there were 18 interventions and 12,000 troops per year, on average, during the period 1886-1990 against striking workers, urban riots, etc. This is detailed in my 1995 article mentioned above on *Internal Military Interventions in the United States*. Systematic data for other countries or for the U.S. in the years since 1990 do not seem to be available.

Discussion of the internal culture of war remains a **taboo topic** even now as we enter the 21st Century. At the level of contemporary diplomatic discourse the existence of the taboo is clear. Nation states consider that internal military intervention is a matter that is not appropriate for inter-governmental forums such as the United Nations. In fact, a special article was included in the UN Charter that forbids the UN from discussing the internal affairs of Member States:

> "Article 2.7: Nothing contained in the present Charter shall authorize the United Nations to intervene in matters which are essentially within the domestic jurisdiction of any state...."

I was reminded of this taboo when, in 1999, the European Union demanded that all reference to the culture of war must be removed from the culture of peace resolution that was eventually adopted by the UN General Assembly.

Extreme examples of the taboo during the 20th Century are provided by Nazi Germany and Soviet Russia during the 1930's. Each had extensive systems of *internal* prison camps that could not be discussed publicly in those countries. Instead, all attention was focused on battles of the military against *external* enemies.

A less extreme example, but no less instructive, is the McCarthy period of U.S. history as described in my history of internal U.S. military interventions. The emphasis on the military buildup during the Cold War, the labeling of an *external* enemy and the claims of extensive spying for this enemy functioned as the cover for *internal* repression of a militant trade union movement influenced by communist ideology, a repression that most of the media was afraid to discuss.

The example given here from the United States regarding taboos against discussion of the internal culture of war could be multiplied by examples in other regions, and readers from Latin America and Eastern Europe will have no difficulty in recognizing this dynamic in their recent history.

The contemporary taboo is not only at the diplomatic and political levels, but extends into the mass media and academic institutions. For example, the analysis of U.S. internal military interventions in my 1995 article in the *Journal of Peace Research*, points out the lack of attention to this topic:

> "The unchanging rate of internal military intervention in the USA and the lack of attention to such intervention in the literature on war and peace are in striking contrast to the rapid changes in other aspects of war and peace. It is argued here that this reflects an oversight which

peace researchers and activists should address in the coming years."

Since the paper was published in 1995, there is still very little attention to this topic. During the intervening twelve years, there have been only four academic references to it according to the Social Science Citation Index, even though it was published in a prestigious journal that one would expect relevant researchers to read.

The media and academia have also paid little attention to a recent example of internal military intervention: the deployment of troops in New Orleans following hurricane Katrina. Jeremy Scahill (2007) in *Blackwater: The Rise of the World's Most Powerful Mercenary Army* (2007) has described how these troops included mercenaries of the Blackwater Company, better known for its use by the U.S. government as a mercenary force in Iraq.

There are many studies in the literature of military science, political science and sociology on the relation of internal and external conflict and intervention, such as the theory that governments faced with internal conflicts may provoke foreign wars as a diversion and as a way of unifying the population around a common enemy. For example, Quincy Wright remarked in his monumental book, *A Study of War* (1942) that wars or the preparations for them have often been used by governments as instruments for dealing with internal disorders. However, with few exceptions the studies of the relation of internal and external conflict tend to avoid reference to internal military interventions in so-called "democratic states". Nor do they point out that "democratic" political leaders consider the military, over the long term, as essential to their maintenance of internal power. Nor do they ask about the relative importance of internal and external functions of war throughout history.

I have argued that the taboo holds among researchers because if they challenge the dominant culture of war, they could endanger their academic careers. In this regard, see the case of David Abraham described in Wiener (2005), *Historians in Trouble: Plagiarism, Fraud and Politics in the Ivory Tower*. As pointed out recently in my Letter to My Academic Friends (2007), most academics contribute to the culture of war either consciously or unconsciously:

> "Academia, as a general rule, is an integral and essential part of the dominant culture of our society, the culture of war. To promote the culture of peace within academia, it is necessary first to free oneself from its prejudices and perspectives, and second to risk one's career by speaking and writing the truth which, in the past, has destroyed the careers of some of the best progressive academicians. Failure to free oneself from these prejudices and perspectives, runs the risk of contributing to the maintenance of the culture of war, either consciously or unconsciously."

The test of a taboo is the punishment that results when the taboo is broken. Take, for example, the taboo against discussing the internal culture of war in socialist countries. Although Marx and Engels were explicit about the use of the military to maintain internal power, Marxist writers of the Twentieth Century, for the most part, no longer dealt with the question of internal war. How else should we explain this except that the 20th Century states run by Communist Parties were themselves maintained by the internal use of military force and to discuss this fact would have been politically dangerous inside those countries and politically embarrassing for Communist Parties outside. As for "democratic countries" such as the United States, many academic critics of the McCarthy era were silenced or fled the country, some going to settle in Canada.

A more subtle way to enforce the taboo was employed during the Reagan administration of the United States during the 1980's. Academics who dared to mention "social class" in their research were denied grants by the major source of grants in the country, the National Institutes of Health. In particular, grants requests were not considered if they involved "studies of large scale social conditions or problems, social class and groups and their interrelations".

The exploitation of the culture of war involves not only exploitation of people, but also **exploitation of the environment**. In recent years everyone has become more aware of the dangers of environmental pollution, with special attention to carbon emissions which have increased atmospheric carbon dioxide and resulted in global warming. This is also related to the loss of the world's forests which redress the problem by removing carbon dioxide from the atmosphere. Insufficient attention has been paid, however, to the great environmental destruction and pollution caused by military activity.

Historically, military-related activity has been one of the primary causes of deforestation. This was already evident in ancient times as described above in the case of Greece and Rome. More recently, the British Empire was a major destroyer of forests, as described for India in an article by Budholai (available on the Internet):

> "The early days of British rule in India were days of plunder of natural resources. They

started exploiting the rich resources present in India by employing the policy of imperialism. By around 1860, Britain had emerged as the world leader in deforestation, devastation its own woods and the forests in Ireland, South Africa and northeastern United States to draw timber for shipbuilding, iron-smelting and farming. Upon occasion, the destruction of forests was used by the British to symbolize political victory. Thus, the early nineteenth century, and following its defeat of the Marathas, the East India Company razed to the ground teak plantation in Ratnagiri nurtured and grown by the legendary Maratha Admiral Kanhoji Angre. There was a total indifference to the needs of the forest conservancy. They caused a fierce onslaught on Indian Forests. The onslaught on the forests was primarily because of the increasing demand for military purposes, for British navy, for local construction (such as roads and railways), supply of teak and sandalwood for export trade and extension of agriculture in order to supplement revenue."

I have not been able to find precise evidence of the environmental damage caused by the contemporary American Empire, but the following description of military pollution by Schmidt (2004) gives some idea of the problem which includes contamination of the land by poisonous chemicals as well as air pollution:

"Preparing for war is a heavily industrialized mission that generates fuel spills, hazardous waste, and air pollution. The DOD owns more than 10% of the 1,240 sites currently on the National Priorities List, and has estimated the cost of cleaning up these sites at approximately $9.7 billion. In addition to lead and a variety of solvents, training facilities release munitions constituents including perchlorate (a thyroid toxicant), RDX (an explosive compound and neurotoxicant), and TNT (an explosive compound linked to anemia and altered liver function).

Nearly 1 in 10 Americans live within 10 miles of a DOD Superfund site—a sometimes perilous proximity. The Massachusetts Military Reservation, for instance, a 34-square-mile multi-use training facility in Cape Cod, is slowly leaching solvents, jet fuel, RDX, and perchlorate into the area's sole aquifer, a drinking water source for up to 500,000 people at the height of tourist season.

Military aircraft from DOD facilities also generate noise and air pollution. For instance, in 1996, the most recent year for which data are available, more than 50,000 military flights contributed to the heavy air traffic over Washington, D.C. According to the Democratic Committee on Energy and Commerce, these flights emitted 75 tons of nitrogen oxides and volatile organic compounds, which generate smog. In 1999, the Sierra Army Depot, located 55 miles northeast of Reno, was California's leading air polluter, according to the EPA Toxics Release Inventory. The base released some 5.4 million pounds of toxic chemicals that year, including aluminum, copper, and zinc fumes."

Military testing and seeding with anti-personnel mines and unexploded or spent ammunition such as cluster bombs and depleted uranium have rendered large tracts of land around the world uninhabitable and unapproachable. I have not been able to find any full accounting of this. However, we know that many people, often children, are still being injured by anti-personnel mines, cluster bomb fragments and other ammunition around the world. Furthermore, any seasoned traveler will have encountered zones that are "off limits" because of military use, often because they have been used for target practice and weapons testing and still contain live ammunition. In addition, does anyone know how much of the world's land is now contaminated with so much radiation from the disposal of radioactive waste or from accident nuclear explosions such as that of Chernobyl that the land will not be habitable for hundreds or thousands of years?

Of course, the above damage is dwarfed by what would happen to the environment if even a small fraction of today's nuclear weapons were used in a nuclear war. At the height of the Cold War, scientific calculations were made showing that the world would enter a "nuclear winter" caused by the clouds from such war, not to mention the lethal levels of radioactivity that would result. It is frightening to realize how close we have come to such a nuclear war. Several years ago, an article on the Culture of Peace News Network described how a Soviet colonel saved the world from a nuclear holocaust when all the signals required him to fire the Soviet nuclear arsenal (http://cpnn-world.org/cgi-bin/read/articlepage.cgi?ViewArticle=175). In recent years, this topic is rarely mentioned despite the fact that the same potential for nuclear destruction remains on attack-alert ready for deployment (another taboo?). One recent study does deal with this in detail, however, the book by Lloyd J. Dumas (1999), *Lethal Arrogance: Human*

Fallibility and Dangerous Technologies, which shows how nuclear war and nuclear accidents continue to be great risks.

4. *Prisons and penal systems*

Prisons and legal and penal systems are an integral part of the internal culture of war. One way to measure their extent is the rate of imprisonment. At the present time, here are figures from the countries with the highest levels, as published on the website of The International Centre for Prison Studies of Kings College, London :

> "By far, the largest prison population is that of the United States at 2,293,157, which is also the highest per capita rate at 756 per 100,000 population. Russia is second with 629. Although China has the second largest prison population at 1,565,771, its per capita rate, 119 per 100,000, is much less because of the fact that its population is so much greater."

Criminal justice systems are heavily biased by race and social class. For example, the imprisonment rate for African-Americans in the United States is ten times higher than for whites. Punishment of law-breakers from the ruling class is much lighter than those from lower classes, and the laws themselves are written in such a way that theft and other crimes by lower classes may be deemed legal for the ruling class. An example is the so-called "Savings-and-Loan Scandal" in the United States in which hundreds of billions of dollars were stolen, but with very few convictions or imprisonments as a result. One of the accused who did not go to prison was the Neil Bush, son of one President and brother of another.

Western penal systems and criminal justice systems continue to be based on principles that have hardly changed from Biblical times: "an eye for an eye and a tooth for a tooth". Criticizing this approach, Mahatma Gandhi stated that "an eye for an eye makes the whole world blind." The principles are so widely accepted that it was very revealing for many of us in the United Nations when South Africa used a different approach in their Truth and Reconciliation Commission (TRC) after the overthrow of Apartheid. The TRC, under the leadership of Nobel Peace Laureate Bishop Desmond Tutu, gave those accused of crimes under Apartheid the option of confession, reparation, forgiveness and rehabilitation. His book, (Tutu, 1999) is "must-reading." In the light of the TRC and other similar approaches, many have criticized Western systems of justice for failing to provide reparation to victims, who are usually left out of the process, or procedures for confession, forgiveness and rehabilitation for the perpetrators of crime.

Capital punishment in the Western systems of criminal justice gives the state the right to murder within the country just as war establishes the right of the state to murder in other countries. Although capital punishment has recently been abolished in Europe, it continues to be practiced in the United States and many other countries.

Legal systems and punishment for disobedience of the law in the bourgeois democracies are designed, above all, to protect private property, and especially the property of the state. This has been true since the beginning of the recorded history of the state. As Leslie A. White (1959) describes in *The Evolution of Culture:*

> "As a means of safeguarding the property foundations of civil society, the state punished theft with severity. Among the Aztecs thieves were enslaved. Petty theft in the Inca state was punished by flogging; theft from the state was punished by death. The Ganda killed a thief if caught in the act; otherwise he was mutilated. In the great urban cultures of the Bronze Age death or mutilation was the usual punishment for theft. Whether drastic punishment acted as a deterrent or not is a question for which we have no adequate answer. But whether it did or did not, it was employed for this purpose. And the frequently lethal reprisals imposed by the state certainly kept many persons from committing the offense a second time."

White makes clear that property law was an invention of the state, because there was no such practice before then: "the economic systems of primitive society place human relationships - human rights and human welfare - above property relations."

5. The military-industrial complex

Over the past century, state militarism has been greatly expanded and strengthened by its alliance with a major branch of industry, the military-industrial complex. As military expenditures have increased, the military-industrial complex has become engaged with the state as a powerful lobby for the maintenance and strengthening of military force and the culture of war that goes with it.

In the United States it has become such an integral part of government that it has come to be called the "military-industrial-congressional complex". An especially authoritative description comes from Chuck Spinney who worked in the U.S. Department of Defense Office of Program Analysis and Evaluation and who made a report in 1982 on the procurement of complex and expensive weapon systems. In the following extract from a television interview by the American journalist Bill Moyers (2002), he explains how Congressmen build their political power base by increasing military production in their home districts:

> "SPINNEY: [The military-industrial-congressional complex] is the product of a long-term evolution that occurred in the 40 years of Cold War. If you think about it those 40 years were a very unique period in our nation's history. Now what happened was during that period the different players in the military industrial Congressional complex basically fine-tuned their bureaucratic behavior to exist in that environment..."
>
> "MOYERS: Tell me how members of Congress benefit from increasing costs like this, driving weapons systems that the country doesn't need, spending money that puts us deeper and deeper in deficit. How does Congress gain?
>
> SPINNEY: They gain because they get money flowing to their Congressional districts. It's in the way Congress gains from controlling the federal budget. They get money flowing to the districts, that helps build your power bases."

There is a particular irony about the history of the term, "military-industrial complex". It was made famous by the farewell speech of American President Dwight Eisenhower in 1961. The speech was written by

Eisenhower's speechwriter Malcolm Moos who, earlier that year had prepared a memo for the President stating that the top hundred defense contractors employed 1,400 retired military officers and that "For the first time in its history, the United States has a permanent war-based industry." According to one account, Eisenhower looked at the draft of his farewell speech and told Moos that he disagreed with it, demanding that he write another kind of speech. After all, Eisenhower's fame came from his career as a military general in charge of Allied forces in World War II. But all of the other Presidential staff members had left since it was the end of his Presidency, and they had taken jobs (guess where!) with the military industry. So when Moos refused to write a different speech, Eisenhower had no other speechwriter to turn to. Unable to write his own speech, Eisenhower had to read the one written by Moos. Moos had been an academic and professor prior to the Eisenhower years, and later he became the President of the University of Minnesota.

Back in the 1980's it was my opinion that the Soviet Union did not have a military-industrial complex, but subsequent revelations showed that this was mistaken. Its existence became evident when Gorbachev attempted to convert military industry to civilian production as a way to avoid the impending crash of the Soviet economy. As explained at a briefing at the United Nations, November 1, 1990 by Ednan Agaev, head of the Division of International Security Issues, Department of International Organization of the Soviet Ministry of Foreign Affairs, the Ministry of Defense refused to provide the Ministry of Foreign Affairs with any information about defense industrial plants. When Agaev reported this to Gorbachev, he was told that there was nothing that could be done about it.

As Spinney describes above in the Moyers interview, the military-industrial-congressional complex has become a driving force for the culture of war in and of itself, as it has come to provide the power base for the political leadership in the United States and perhaps other countries as well. In this sense, one needs to add this "use" for the culture of war to the other uses that have persisted since the dawn of civilization: conquest, defense and internal control.

The military-industrial complex has reinforced the culture of war in smaller countries as well. Even the European countries of the Netherlands, Sweden and Italy are among the major exporters of armaments, ranking ahead of China. Putting "Sweden" and "military-industrial complex" into an Internet search engine revealed the following section of an article entitled Democracy and Globalization in which Professor Lars Ingelstam (2000), Institute for TEMA, Linköping University, Sweden explained how the Swedish government supports military spending as an essential component of the national economy:

> "... a recent Swedish public inquiry on information technology found that the market for high technology within the defence sector was likely to decline. But instead of noting that probable development plainly and, one would have thought, with a degree of satisfaction that it was linked to a reduced risk of war, the commission expressed concern that the resulting 'loss of competence... will create problems for related production in such areas as civil aeronautics, high-speed electronics, advanced MMI and control systems, etc.,'
>
> The commission concluded that it was necessary for the government to guarantee an annual

purchase-volume of at least one billion Swedish kronor for affected industries."

6. The drugs-for-guns trade

Another taboo topic is the long and important history of the drug trade in the culture of war. This relationship goes back at least to the colonial wars, with the most dramatic being the Opium Wars by which the Americans and Europeans subjugated and exploited China. Alcohol was often used in colonial domination and genocide, for example the European subjugation of the native peoples of North America.

One does not usually think of the drug trade in conjunction with the military-industrial complex, but in the following account, it should become evident that a major part of the drug trade in recent years has become, in effect, a military-industrial complex that is illegal and yet engaged by secret military and quasi-military services of governments.

Many in my generation became aware of the drugs-for-guns trade during the Vietnam War. Air America, a company established and controlled by U.S. Central Intelligence Agency, flew sorties between Laos and Hong Kong, said to be carrying heroin one way and guns and ammunition for anti-communist Laos tribesmen the other way. By selling the heroin to Mafia-related distributors in Hong Kong, the CIA was able to finance a secret war without having to obtain funds from the U.S. Congress. The size of Air America was enormous. It was, in effect, a secret military-industrial complex. According to the following information at www.vietnam.ttu.edu/airamerica/best on the Internet, it had the largest airline fleet in the world at that time.

> "Air America was owned by the CIA and played a leading role in logistic air support of the CIA's forces in Laos from 1959 to 1974 ... By 1966 Air America had almost 6,000 employees. At its peak in 1970, Air America had the largest airline fleet in the world, in terms of numbers of aircraft owned, although a lot of these aircraft were small or helicopters. Air America operated up to 30,000 flights per month by 1970."

The drug trade was managed through secret collaboration between the government and the Mafia. Similar arrangements between the CIA and the Mafia have been documented with regard to the repeated attempts to assassinate Fidel Castro, and a particularly remarkable exposé is that of Claudia Furiati (1994), *ZR Rifle: The Plot to Kill Kennedy and Castro*, based on files from the Cuban State Security Department about the collaboration between the CIA and the Mafia in the assassination of President John F. Kennedy.

The trade of drugs for guns surfaced again during American support of Afghan rebels against the Soviet Union in Afghanistan, as documented, for example, by Alfred McCoy (1997) in The Progressive, *Drug fallout: the CIA's Forty Year Complicity in the Narcotics Trade*:

> "[Soon after CIA operations began against the Soviets in Afghanistan] the Pakistan-Afghanistan borderlands became the world's top heroin producer, supplying 60 percent of U.S. demand ... CIA assets again controlled this heroin trade. As the Mujahideen guerrillas seized territory inside Afghanistan, they ordered peasants to plant opium as a revolutionary tax. Across the border in Pakistan, Afghan leaders

and local syndicates under the protection of Pakistan Intelligence operated hundreds of heroin laboratories. During this decade of wide-open drug-dealing, the U.S. Drug Enforcement Agency in Islamabad failed to instigate major seizures or arrests ... In 1995, the former CIA director of the Afghan operation, Charles Cogan, admitted the CIA had indeed sacrificed the drug war to fight the Cold War. 'Our main mission was to do as much damage as possible to the Soviets. We didn't really have the resources or the time to devote to an investigation of the drug trade'"

The drugs-for-guns trade was especially blatant during the Contra War run covertly by the CIA against Nicaragua. It was said that planes flew regularly between small airports in Central America and the United States, carrying guns one way to the Contras and cocaine the other way that was transferred to Mafia distributors in the US. It may be assumed that many of the documents shredded by Marine Colonel Oliver North to avoid investigation in the "Iran-Contra Scandal" were records of the aircraft flights that he managed from the basement of the Reagan White House in Washington. Trying to find public data on this is not easy, however, because of the fears and taboos involved.

Perhaps no topic has been more taboo in recent years than the drugs-for-guns trade. One exposé in the New York Times on April 10, 1988 mentions the trade in Vietnam, Afghanistan and the Contra War, but it stops short of mentioning direct involvement in the drug trade by the U.S. government and CIA. Another series of articles in the San Jose Mercury News in 1996 was more explicit about government involvement, but it resulted in a wave of criticism and retractions. The public portions of the trials and hearings on the so-called "Iran-Contra Scandal" omitted discussion of the involvement with drugs, while many portions of their reports remain secret.

A non-governmental organization, the Christic Institute, filed a lawsuit and distributed videos at that time providing documentation of government involvement in drugs for guns, but the videos were sought out and confiscated by the U.S. government, and the organization was destroyed in a bizarre series of court cases and murders which can be tracked by entering "Christic Institute" on an Internet search engine. Perhaps the closest there is to a public record of this issue came from the United States Senate Committee Report on Drugs, Law Enforcement and Foreign Policy (1986) chaired by Senator John F. Kerry, from which the following quotation is taken:

> "While the contra/drug question was not the primary focus of the investigation, the Subcommittee uncovered considerable evidence relating to the Contra network which substantiated many of the initial allegations laid out before the Committee in the Spring of 1986. On the basis of this evidence, it is clear that individuals who provided support for the Contras were involved in drug trafficking, the supply network of the Contras was used by drug trafficking organizations, and elements of the Contras themselves knowingly received financial and material assistance from drug traffickers. In each case, one or another agency of the U.S. government had information regarding the involvement either while it was occurring, or immediately thereafter."

Among the airports involved in the network was that of Mena, Arkansas, in the United States (many details are available by putting this into an Internet search engine), and that of the ranch of John Hull in Costa Rica. The following information about the latter comes from the Kerry Subcommittee hearings (see above Internet reference):

> "John Hull was a central figure in Contra operations on the Southern Front when they were managed by Oliver North, from 1984 through late 1986. Before that, according to former Costa Rican CIA station chief Thomas Castillo's public testimony, Hull had helped the CIA with military supply and other operations on behalf of the Contras. In addition, during the same period, Hull received $10,000 a month from Adolfo Calero of the FDN--at North's direction..."
>
> "Five witnesses testified that Hull was involved in cocaine trafficking: Floyd Carlton, Werner Lotz, Jose Blandon, George Morales, and Gary Betzner. Betzner was the only witness who testified that he was actually present to witness cocaine being loaded onto planes headed for the United States in Hull's presence.
>
> Lotz said that drugs were flown into Hull's ranch, but that he did not personally witness the flights. He said he heard about the drug flights from the Colombian and Panamanian pilots who allegedly flew drugs to Hull's airstrips. Lotz described the strips as 'a stop for refuel basically. The aircraft would land, there would be fuel waiting for them, and then would depart. They would come in with weapons and drugs.'"

Drugs continue to arrive in the U.S. as part of U.S. military missions in the 21st Century. Cocaine comes from Colombia where U.S. forces are secretly involved in the so-called "Plan Colombia" and heroin comes from Afghanistan where opium remains a major cash crop in the areas contested by NATO forces on one side and the Taliban on the other. The effect of drugs on the streets of the United States and other countries is a terrible side of the culture of war. Not only are many people addicted, but there is a very high murder rate associated with drug distribution and many of the two million people now in prison in the United States are there under conviction for offenses related to the drug trade.

On a global scale, the trade in narcotics, often associated with gun-running, is one of the largest industries in the world. The United Nations World Drug Report of 2005 estimated the total retail value of the world narcotics trade at 321 billion dollars. This may well be an underestimate since the trade is illegal, cloaked in secrecy, and often, it may be assumed, protected by government agencies.

Much of the violence at a local level is a result of the drug trade and the closely related illegal trade in guns. Drug cartels target for assassination those who threaten their trade, and local dealers engage in "turf wars" with rival dealers. This violence often takes on the characteristics of feuding and can be considered its modern equivalent, as each murder requires vengeance and another murder. Since all of this takes place under the moral umbrella of a criminal justice system based on the principle of "an eye for an eye", the entire process is best understood as an integral part of the culture of war.

7. Authoritarian control

The authoritarian control associated with the culture of war has continued from the beginning of recorded history up until the present time. There were many extreme cases during the 20th Century with Hitler's Germany and Stalin's Soviet Union being among the most brutal. The list of dictatorial regimes is extensive and applies to all regions of the world. These regimes have been associated with all the aspects of the culture of war including use of enemy images, intensive armament and military training, control of the mass media with propaganda and secrecy, violations of human rights, prison labor camps and male domination. The role of the arts and religion has been divided under dictatorships, some being enlisted in support of authoritarian regimes, and some valiantly and often tragically, opposed.

At the same time there have been powerful movements of democratization, including both violent revolutions (which have usually produced new authoritarian regimes) and nonviolent revolutions such as those in South Africa, Eastern Europe and the Philippines. And it has become fashionable to speak and act in support of democracy, including at the United Nations.

Does this mean that the nation states of the world are turning away from the culture of war and towards a culture of peace? Some would answer this in the affirmative. Many political scientists have claimed that in recent times, "democracies do not make war on other democracies". Their data are impressive, but open to criticism. First of all, they tend to emphasize open warfare and to avoid analysis of covert war. For example, they conveniently ignore covert warfare such as the American Contra War against Nicaragua mentioned above and the overthrow of the socialist government headed by Salvador Allende in Chile. Similarly, they do not consider the embargo that the United States has imposed for many decades on neighboring Cuba as an act of war, despite the fact that in many respects it resembles the sieges that have been an essential part of warfare since the beginning of recorded history. Second, there is a tendency to use narrow definitions of democracy with criteria that derive from the political systems of developed Northern states, multi-party elections, etc. Hence, they ignore the above-mentioned actions against Cuba and Nicaragua by maintaining that those countries were not "democracies."

Despite the shortcomings of the analysis that "democracies do not make war on other democracies" it reflects an important advance of consciousness towards a culture of peace. It can be restated in the form "When bourgeois democracies want to make war on other bourgeois democracies, they are forced to do so in secret because their citizenry would not approve it." The fact that governments are increasingly required by their citizenry to justify war and to obtain their permission indicates that there is an increasing anti-war consciousness which has considerable influence in the political process.

The reaction to the launching of two recent wars led by the United States against Iraq reflects the increased anti-war sentiment among the citizenry. It has been argued that the first Gulf War was kept very brief, without an invasion of Iraq, because of mounting citizen opposition by major religious and labor organizations, as well as rapidly-developing Congressional opposition to the war. For the second Gulf War, the U.S. went to the United Nations to get approval and failed. At that time there was an unprecedented outpouring of people onto the streets in opposition to the impending war with over 10 million people marching, including in the major cities of America's allies. One of the reasons that the United States government has involved itself in the illegal drug trade in conjunction with wars in Iran, Afghanistan and Nicaragua has been its inability to obtain adequate financing through the legal means of Congressional approval. This is rather ironic in view of the U.S. Congress complicity in the "Military-Industrial-Congressional Complex" as described earlier.

But are democracies really democratic?

In favor of democracy, voting rights have gradually been extended over the course of centuries. For example, in the early days of bourgeois democracy in the United States, voting rights were confined to men who were land-owners. Women and men who did not own land were excluded, and, of course, slaves were excluded. By the 1830's in most states all free men were allowed to vote, removing restrictions based on property and religion (at first voting was denied to those from religions other than Protestant). In 1870, following the Civil War, the Constitution was amended to allow African-Americans the right to vote, a right that has yet to be fully respected. And in 1920, a further Constitutional amendment granted women the right to vote. Both of the latter two advances came after long struggle by the Abolitionist Movement against slavery and the Movement for Women's Suffrage. Women's suffrage was first attained in a large country in New Zealand and Australia in 1893 and 1894 respectively, followed by Finland in 1906. In England women gained the right to vote in 1918, while in France and Italy it was not attained until after World War II. In most other countries of the world, women's voting came after World War II, and women still cannot vote in Saudi Arabia (Kuwait allowed women to vote in 2005).

When we drafted the culture of peace document for the United Nations, we avoided the term "democracy" and spoke instead of "democratic participation". On the one hand, this was to avoid dealing with the fact that certain authoritarian regimes such as the Peoples Democratic Republic of Korea include the word "democratic" in the names of their countries. On the other hand, it enabled us to emphasize "participation" as an essential part of democracy which often seems to be lost in practice.

Are the two-party systems of countries like the United States and parliamentary systems like those of Europe truly based on citizen participation? While it is true that there are regular elections and the voters have a choice between several parties, does that mean that the governments that are elected truly represent the interests of the citizenry? Consider the Marxist critique made over a century ago by Lenin in *The State and Revolution.* He begins by quoting Kautsky that "the modern representative state is an instrument of exploitation of wage-labor by capital." and he goes on to say that bourgeois democracy is the "best possible political shell for capitalism" :

> "... the omnipotence of 'wealth' is more certain in a democratic republic [because] it does not depend on defects in the political machinery or on the faulty political shell of capitalism. A democratic republic is the best possible political shell for capitalism, and, therefore, once capital has gained possession of this very best shell ... it establishes its power so securely, so firmly, that no change of persons, institutions or parties in the bourgeois-democratic republic can shake it."

Taking seriously the Marxist criticisms of bourgeois democracy, one cannot help but recognize that wealth continues to determine most "democratic" elections. This comes at a moment of history when nothing is more evident than the increasing gap between rich and poor, both within and between nations. The role of television in the modern election campaign has greatly increased the importance of wealth; campaigns for President of the United States cost hundreds of millions of dollars, while campaigns for Congress or city mayors now cost millions. A large proportion of the members of the U.S. Congress are themselves millionaires.

The Marxist critique is also supported by the fact that democratic elections are aborted or overthrown by the major powers when governments are elected that do not support the international capitalist class. Hence, when socialists were elected in Chile under President Allende, the United States government joined with international capitalist enterprises such as IT&T to subvert the government and bring to power the military dictatorship of Pinochet. When Islamists were elected in Algeria in 1992, European states tacitly supported a military coup to overturn the election results. Since Hamas scored an electoral victory in Palestine at the beginning of 2006, the Europeans, Americans and Israelis have done everything possible to ensure that they could not govern. Although denied by the United States, many people around the world are convinced by the evidence that a recent coup d'état was supported by the Americans to overthrown the election results in Venezuela that brought Hugo Chavez to power.

Perhaps most important of all, there is no pretext in the capitalist states that economic decisions are made with democratic participation. Elected congresses and parliaments do not interfere in the "internal matters" of the capitalist enterprise which, after all, is where the exploitation and transfer of wealth occurs both within the country concerned and abroad. Decisions are made by the owners and shareholders of enterprises, not by the workers or by their elected representatives in government. So-called "free enterprise" in this sense is enterprise that is "free" for the capitalists to rule without question or challenge. Only socialists, and then only rarely, have experimented with workers' elections of their management.

Finally, democracy cannot function if the electorate is not aware of what its elected officials are doing? An increasing proportion of government actions are cloaked in secrecy, under claims of "national defense". This is a fundamental question to be addressed in the following section on control of information.

It is important to distinguish between democracy at the level of the state and democracy at the local level. Very often, at the local level, there is much more citizen participation and free flow of information. For this, and other related reasons, it can be said that at the present moment of history local government is much closer to a culture of peace, while the state is more engaged in the culture of war.

8. Control of information

The most significant development in the culture of war over the course of history has been the increasing importance of the control of information. In parallel with the developments of the printing press, the telephone and radio, television and now Internet, the control of these media has been crucial for the maintenance or changing of political power, no less for bourgeois democracy than for authoritarian regimes. We have already mentioned one example: the important role of television in electoral campaigns, and how it provides an ever-increasing advantage to those who are wealthy or have access to wealth.

In recent years control of the media has greatly reinforced the culture of war of the state and military-industrial complex. Never before in history has there been such a concentration of communication power in the hands of a few multi-national corporations, Most media in the United States, for example, are now in the hands of five multi-national corporations. There was popular resistance to this a few years ago, but the media monopolies were supported by the responsible government agency, the Federal Communication Commission (FCC). The FCC was stocked with appointments of the Bush administration and headed by the son of General Colin Powell, the Secretary of State in the Bush administration who initiated the war in Iraq.

At the international level, a particularly revealing moment occurred when UNESCO considered implementation of the proposals of the International Commission for the Study of Communication Problems (UNESCO 1980). This is usually called the MacBride report after its chairman, the Nobel Peace Laureate Sean MacBride. The MacBride report recognized the dominance of Northern media and called for the "democratization of communication at national and international levels":

> [page 111]: "We can sum up by saying that in the communication industry there are a relatively small number of predominant corporations which integrate all aspects of production and distribution, which are based in the leading developed countries and which have become transnational in their operations. Concentration of resources and infrastructures is not only a growing trend, but also a worrying phenomenon which may adversely affect the

freedom and democratization of communication..."

[page 253]: "Our conclusions are founded on the firm conviction that communication is a basic individual right, as well as a collective one required by all communities and nations. Freedom of information -- and, more specifically the right to seek, receive and impart information -- is a fundamental human right; indeed, a prerequisite for many others. The inherent nature of communication means that its fullest possible exercise and potential depend on the surrounding political, social and economic conditions, the most vital of these being democracy within countries and equal, democratic relations between them. It is in this context that the democratization of communication at national and international levels, as well as the larger role of communication in democratizing society, acquires utmost importance."

When it looked like they could not block implementation of the MacBride Report, the United States and the United Kingdom withdrew from UNESCO, effectively removing a majority of its operational budget and putting enormous pressure on their allies that remained in the organization. When I was at UNESCO in the 1990s there was no question but that this topic had become taboo for the organization. And meanwhile the concentration of the power of media in the hands of the wealthy continues to grow. As A. J. Liebling once wrote, "Freedom of the press is guaranteed only to those who own one".

And perhaps never before in history has there been so much secrecy in government. Even though the functions of secrecy are often to hide incompetence and corruption, it is usually justified by the state in terms of "national security" - i.e. the culture of war. To illustrate the extent of secrecy, here is a small article clipped from the May 14 1997 issue of the International Herald Tribune:

> "Washington - Representative David Skaggs, Democrat of Colorado, was quizzing the head of administrative services at the CIA about classified material a while ago. How much, he asked, did the agency spend each year on classification?
>
> Well, the official said, that information is classified. Mr Skaggs persisted: "Why is that?" he asked. "I'll have to get back to you on that" he recalled the official saying. He's still waiting.
>
> In the federal government, there is perhaps nothing so wonderfully Byzantine as a secret. You literally don't know what you don't know. And if you did know what you don't know, you still couldn't know it. That's called the need to know, and unless you have it, you may never know.
>
> But what we do know, courtesy of the Information Security Oversight Office of the National Archives, is that the government - except the CIA - spent $5.23 billion on classification last year.
>
> Mr Skaggs would like to demystify democracy by shrinking the number of secrets, and hopes

> that holding down classification costs will cause the amount of classified material to decline. (WP)"

As the article points out, it is difficult to know how much secrecy there is, because "you don't know what you don't know." However, there is every indication that the amount of secrecy in the U.S. government has increased since 1994. We have already indicated how secrecy was used by the U.S. government to avoid being implicated in the guns for drugs trade during the Contra War, and we can only assume that many other illegal actions related to the culture of war have similarly been hidden from the general public. Nor is the problem confined to the United States. Recent revelations about the secret complicity of European governments with illegal CIA rendition and torture show that other countries keep extensive "national security" secrets as well.

The control of the mass media by a few major multinational corporations plays into the hands of governmental secrecy and propaganda. To some extent media propaganda supports militarism because of a community of interest between the media executives and the government. This seems to have been the case to a great extent in the extraordinary support given by the American mass media to the war in Iraq during its initial years. This support has been documented by the journalist Bill Moyers, as in the following excerpt from interviews he did with other journalists for his television program, "Buying the War" which was broadcast on PBS April 25, 2007:

> "Four years ago this spring the Bush administration took leave of reality and plunged our country into a war so poorly planned it soon turned into a disaster. The story of how high officials misled the country has been told. But

they couldn't have done it on their own; they needed a compliant press, to pass on their propaganda as news and cheer them on ... As the war rages into its fifth year, we look back at those months leading up to the invasion, when our press largely surrendered its independence and skepticism to join with our government in marching to war."

"... BILL MOYERS: What did you think? What does that say to you? That dissent is unpatriotic?

PHIL DONOHUE: Well, not only unpatriotic, but it's not good for business ..."

"NORM SOLOMAN I think these executives were terrified of being called soft on terrorism. They absolutely knew that the winds were blowing at hurricane force politically and socially in the United States. And rather than stand up for journalism, they just blew with the wind ..."

"DAN RATHER: Fear is in every newsroom in the country. And fear of what? Well, it's the fear it's a combination of: if you don't go along to get along, you're going to get the reputation of being a troublemaker. There's also the fear that, you know, particularly in networks, they've become huge, international conglomerates. They have big needs, legislative needs, repertory needs in Washington. Nobody has to send you a memo to tell you that that's the case ... You know. And that puts a seed in your mind; of well, if you stick your neck out, if you take the risk of going against the grain with your reporting, is anybody going to back you up?"

In a companion broadcast Bill Moyers recalls the role of American media propaganda in earlier wars:

> "The Spanish-American War is often seen as a conflict almost initiated and fed by propaganda. Publisher of THE NEW YORK JOURNAL Randolph Hearst is commonly believed to have told a reporter in Cuba, "You furnish the pictures, I'll provide the war." Regardless of the veracity of that tale, Hearst's claim in the press that Spanish mines had sunk the Maine, pushed the nation toward war. His paper's notorious and ugly characterization of the Spanish and generous helpings of melodrama and sentiment became known as 'Yellow Journalism.'
>
> World War I marked the American government's first official foray into creating propaganda. In order to jumpstart enlistment and sell war bonds to a somewhat isolationist public, President Wilson formed the Committee of Public Information. The CPI produced posters, films and other material that equated the American cause with democracy, hearth and home. American propaganda took its tone from British and French efforts which stressed the brutality of "The Hun" and the "rape" of neutral Belgium. Worries about immigration and European revolutions became prominent in government propaganda in the post-war Red Scare."

To some extent media propaganda is directed by secret government infiltration of the media. Only once has the U.S. Congress held substantial hearings into government infiltration and manipulation of the media. This was the 1975 hearings of the Senate Intelligence Committee, called the Church Committee after its chairman, Senator Frank Church. Few people would know about the Church Committee hearings were it not for an article by the reporter Carl Bernstein, although Bernstein's report was not accepted for publication by "main-line" media and he was only able to publish it in the alternative press, the Rolling Stone Magazine (see Bernstein 1977). The Bernstein article reveals that the Church Committee found extensive secret CIA infiltration of the mass media, including the New York Times, CBS and Time Inc. The data revealed by Bernstein and the Church Committee were only the tip of the iceberg, however. As Bernstein says, the Committee was blocked from going further with its investigation:

> "Despite the evidence of widespread CIA use of journalists, the Senate Intelligence Committee and its staff decided against questioning any of the reporters, editors, publishers or broadcast executives whose relationships with the Agency are detailed in CIA files.
>
> According to sources in the Senate and the Agency, the use of journalists was one of two areas of inquiry which the CIA went to extraordinary lengths to curtail. The other was the Agency's continuing and extensive use of academics for recruitment and information gathering purposes.
>
> In both instances, the sources said, former directors Colby and Bush and CIA special counsel Mitchell Rogovin were able to convince key members of the committee that full inquiry

> or even limited public disclosure of the dimensions of the activities would do irreparable damage to the nation's intelligence-gathering apparatus, as well as to the reputations of hundreds of individuals."

The mass media, in recent times, has been increasingly used as an important weapon of choice in what is called "psychological warfare." A particularly detailed description is provided by the article *CIA Psychological Warfare Operations: Case Studies in Chile, Jamaica, and Nicaragua* published by the psychologist Fred Landis in Science for the People Magazine, January/February 1982. Unfortunately, the article is not available on the Internet. It is rich in detail, and the following quotation gives only an overview:

> "In the last decade, four American nations have chosen a socialist road to development. -- Chile, Jamaica, Nicaragua, and Grenada. In the first three cases the CIA responded, among other actions by virtually taking over the major newspaper in that country and using it as an instrument of destabilization ..."

> "The appropriation of newspapers by the CIA proceeds through certain discrete, identifiable stages. These include: using an international press association, firing many of the staff, modernizing the physical plant, changing the format of the front page, using subliminal propaganda, assassinating the character of government ministers, promoting a counter-elite to replace the socialist government, spreading disinformation, using divisive propaganda to create artificial conflicts within the society,

> dusting off stock CIA stories and themes, coordinating the propaganda effort with an economic, diplomatic, and paramilitary offensive, and generally following the blueprint for psychological warfare as outlined in the U.S. Army *Field Manual of Psychological Operations.*"

Perhaps the most remarkable aspect of the Landis article are the illustrations from the front pages of newspapers after they are taken over for psychological warfare. They headline stories of atrocities and violence that can only strike fear into the viewer. What is so remarkable is the extent to which these types of themes may be now be found the front pages of major "tabloid" newspapers and the screens of right wing television networks, not only in countries under attack, but in the countries of the North including North America and Europe. In these cases the media has become an agent of psychological warfare that instills a climate of fear in the average citizen, and as it has been said, "fear is the language of empire."

One particular way that the mass media supports the culture of war is to perpetuate the myth that warfare is inevitable because it is part of human nature. For some detail on this, see Adams (1989, 1991).

9. Identification of an "enemy"

Enemy images have been promoted throughout history. After World War II, the main enemy images were those of the Cold War: the enemy of "godless communism" in the West, and the enemy of "capitalist imperialists" in the East. Those of us who opposed the Cold War found ourselves in opposition to an enormously complex propaganda machine that needed an enemy in order to justify national policies.

There was a remarkable moment at the end of the Cold War when, at a summit meeting, the Soviet premier Gorbachev told the American President Reagan that "I am going to deprive you of your enemy." At that point it became urgent for the West that a new enemy had to be found in order to justify the war machine.

The new enemy was found: the Islamic world. In an influential article in the journal *Foreign Affairs,* the Harvard professor Samuel Huntington came up with the phrase "clash of civilizations" that had been developed in his association with CIA think-tanks. And, after a few years, the new enemy image was reinforced by the attacks on the World Trade Center in New York on September 11, 2001.

Under the umbrella of these two sets of over-arching enemy images, there are dozens of other sets of enemy images related to local wars and histories of wars, ranging from Tutsi versus Hutu to Cuba versus the United States.

Enemy images are propagated by the mass media and educational systems, as described in other sections of this book, and they are so pervasive that we come to take them for granted, forgetting how they may have changed from one generation to another and how yesterdays' enemy has become today's ally.

10. Education for a culture of war

Military education has a long and impressive history. Working at UNESCO, my window overlooked the courtyard of Ecole Militaire, the military school where Napoleon was trained in the 18th Century, and each day I watched the various exercises of the young officers as they engaged in horseback riding, volleyball and football, and marching bands with martial music on special occasions. I took photos with the idea to write book someday called "*I was a spy for the culture of peace.*" In fact, the view was not by accident because the great socialist premier of pre-war France, Leon Blum, was on the committee that made the plans for UNESCO after World War II, and he wanted UNESCO functionaries like me to overlook the yard where the young Jewish officer Dreyfus was unfairly court-martialed in 1894.

What I saw in the courtyard of Ecole Militaire was almost identical to what one would have seen in ancient Greece and Rome, which illustrates the universality over time and space of education for military officers. I can imagine that if you could put Julius Caesar, Napoleon and present-day generals together with interpreters in a room, they would understand each other perfectly.

In my scholarly work on internal military interventions, I have been impressed by the high quality of military scholarship, as it seems that military education in the West is seen as an unbroken chain of history going back to Alexander the Great and Julius Caesar. Similarly, as mentioned earlier, it is said that Mao Tse Tung was an avid reader of Sun-zi's *Art of War,* from 2500 years ago.

The military education of officers is reserved for a small elite group of men, although in recent years a few women have been admitted in some countries, with results that have been problematic.

Modern education systems, aside from military education, are formally or informally divided into schools for the elite and schools for ordinary people. Each country has its elite schools, such as Yale and Harvard in the U.S., Oxford and Cambridge in the U.K., the Grandes Écoles in France, etc. Traditionally they were limited to men, and only recently have women been admitted. Elite schools are historically linked to the ruling class and the culture of war and they prepare their students to function in the ruling class. For example, to establish the CIA, it was desired to have a close-knit group of young men from the ruling class who had gone to school together, and for that reason most of the initial generation of CIA officials came from the secret society *Skull and Bones* at Yale University. Significantly, the U.S. Presidential election in 2004 was a choice between two members of *Skull and Bones,* George W. Bush and Bill Kerry.

The elite universities often lead the way in key themes of the culture of war such as racism and genetic determinism. As noted later in the section on racism, in the U.S. it has been Harvard University that has played over the years a leading role in claims of genetic inferiority of African-Americans and socio-biological claims that war is part of human nature.

Ordinary schooling is designed to prepare youth to function well within a culture of war by working obediently within an authoritarian society. An especially insightful critique is that of the Brazilian literacy teacher, Paulo Freire (1968) in *Pedagogy of the Oppressed,* who calls it the "banking concept of education":

> "Education thus becomes an act of depositing, in which the students are the depositories and the teacher is the depositor. Instead of communicating, the teacher issues communiqués and makes deposits which the students patiently receive, memorize, and repeat. This is the

'banking' concept of education, in which the scope of action allowed to the students extends only as far as receiving, filing, and storing the deposits ...."

"It is not surprising that the banking concept of education regards men as adaptable, manageable beings, The more students work at storing the deposits entrusted to them, the less they develop the critical consciousness would result from their intervention in the world. The more completely they accept the passive role imposed on them, the more they tend simply to adapt to the world as it is and to the fragmented view of reality deposited in them.

The capability of banking education to minimize or annul the students' creative power and to stimulate their credulity serves the interests of the oppressors, who care neither to have the world revealed nor to see it transformed. The oppressors use their 'humanitarianism' to preserve a profitable situation. Thus they react almost instinctively against any experiment in education which stimulates the critical faculties and is not content with a partial view of reality but always seeks out the ties which link one point to another and one problem to another.

Indeed, the interests of the oppressors lie in 'changing the consciousness of the oppressed, not the situation which oppresses them;' for the more the oppressed can be led to adapt to that situation, the more easily they can be dominated. To achieve this end, the oppressors use the banking concept of education-- in conjunction with a paternalistic social action apparatus ..."

A perspective remarkably similar to the "banking concept of education" is the "McDonalidization of education." This was supported by the Assistant Director-General for Education at UNESCO, John Daniel (2002) in *Education Today,* the newsletter of UNESCO's Education Sector. Rather than treating education as problem-solving, as proposed by Freire, he treats education as a commodity:

"The hue and cry about the 'McDonaldization' of education should make us reach for our critical faculties. First, despite their ubiquity, McDonald's restaurants account for only a tiny proportion of the food that people eat. Second, McDonald's is successful because people like their food. Third, their secret is to offer a limited range of dishes as commodities that have the same look, taste and quality everywhere.

Commoditization. It's an ugly word that my spellchecker rejects. But it is a key process for bringing prosperity to ordinary people by giving them greater freedom and wider choice. Products that were once hand crafted and expensive become standardized, mass produced and inexpensive. Personal computers and cellular telephones used to be specialized items for the elite. Today they are mass-market consumer items ..."

"What are the implications for education? Is the commoditization of learning material a way to bring education to all? Yes it is, and open universities in a number of countries have shown the way. By developing courseware for large numbers of students they can justify the investment required to produce high quality learning materials at low unit cost. ... We can imagine a future in which teachers and institutions make their courseware and learning materials freely available on the web. Anyone else can translate and adapt them for local use provided they make their new version freely available too. ... The Massachusetts Institute of Technology has shown the way by making its own web materials available free. Let's hope this heralds a worldwide movement to commoditize education for the common good."

A practical result of the tendency toward "banking" or "McDonaldization" of education is the recent U.S. Government program of "No Child Left Behind" which requires standardized tests that each student must pass. This has literally transformed the educational systems of the United States. As described in the following excerpt from a newspaper article by Bacon (2000), this approach has led to a special relationship between the education system and multinational corporations and it has increased rather than decreased the gap between education for the rich and for the poor:

"This the year U.S. schools went test-crazy. By January every state but one had adopted standards for public school students in at least one subject and 41 states had adopted tests to measure student performance.

Promotion from one grade to another, and high school graduation itself, are now often test-determined. Test scores increasingly determine the ranking of schools, the resources available to them, and even control of the local curriculum.

Meanwhile, politicians vie with each other to position themselves as pro-education. This almost obsessive interest in testing is driven by factors ranging from political ambition to a genuine desire for public schools that teach their students. But a big push comes from a much less publicized source -- the testing companies themselves.

Districts and states spend huge sums on testing and standards, money that goes to a few large companies, which also publish school texts. Dominating the field are three big publishers -- McGraw-Hill, Harcourt and Houghton-Mifflin ... Testing brought in an estimated $218.7 million for 1999 according to the Association of American Publishers .... "

"But what do the tests actually measure? And even more important, do standardized tests really improve the quality of education?

Two Ohio mothers say the tests hurt students. 'We used to have a wonderfully rich program in our schools,' says Mary O'Brien, who has five kids in public schools. 'Now it's all oriented to test-taking. They just rank and sort students -- they don't actually teach them much at all.'"

"... an exhaustive study by Youngstown State University Professor Randy Hoover ... found that the poorer the family, the lower the score was likely to be. Schools in affluent neighborhoods do predictably well, and schools in poor, minority neighborhoods don't ...."

"But ranking schools isn't necessarily going to lead to reallocating resources. Next year, promotion to fifth grade in Ohio will depend on passing the reading test. Students who don't pass will be concentrated in schools with the least resources, which will have even greater problems paying for teachers, classrooms and materials to help them catch up.

Furthermore, in many states, school districts that rank low on tests may lose funding, and see students and resources diverted to charter schools. Even pay raises for personnel are being tied to test rankings."

11. Male domination

In a number of domains women have gained more rights in recent times. For example, as we have noted, women have gained the right to vote, there are now more women elected to parliaments and there are now women in military and elite schools although they remain a small minority in most cases. These changes have been achieved through the revolutionary struggles in the 19th and 20th Centuries for women's suffrage.

Although contemporary societies continue to be dominated by men, this domination has diminished in recent years. Women are increasingly involved in the military, with the extreme case being the Israeli Army, although they remain a minority of the officer corps. In political life, there are an increasing number of women elected to leadership positions. As this is being written, the most egregious culture of war, that of Israel against the Palestinians, is under the political leadership of women: Foreign Minister Tzipi Livni of Israel, with the essential support of the Secretaries of State of the United States, Condoleezza Rice and her successor, Hilary Clinton. In the major capitalist enterprises, traditionally dominated by men, there are an increasing number of women in leadership positions. Even among religions, there are a few sects in which women can now become priests, although that is still not the case for some of the largest religious bodies such as the Roman Catholic Church.

The fact that increasing numbers of women are involved in the culture of war is in contradiction to a frequently-stated claim that the culture of war is due primarily to "patriarchy," i.e. male domination. No doubt, male domination is an essential part of the culture of war, but it is only one part and not, by itself, determinant.

Looking back over recorded history, one can see how it has been the culture of war that has perpetuated male domination. Let me start by quoting again the following passage in my study, *Why There Are So Few Women Warriors* (1983):

> "With the advent of internal war, patrilocality, and exogamy, there came a profound shift in male-female relations. The male monopolization of warfare was instituted and extended to hunting (in order to preclude the use of weapons by women) and to the initiation rites of the young (male) warriors. The inequality of power between men and women was institutionalized in a way from which we have never recovered."

The inequality of power between men and women was further strengthened at the advent of the state, in which war played a decisive role. The rulers of the state were those who had been victorious in war, and as a result, from its origins the state has been dominated by men. There have always been a few exceptions. We have already mentioned the Pharaoh Hatshepsut in ancient Egypt. In more recent times, one can point to the long reign of Queen Victoria in England, a period marked by British military domination of an empire on which it was said that "the sun never sets."

The historical examples of women rulers stand out because they have been so few and exceptional. The vast majority of rulers have been men, and it may be assumed that this is related to the primacy of warfare as a function of the state, and the fact that military leaders have always been men.

As for elite education, it is only in the recent past that women have gained entrance:

>   Cambridge Colleges from 1960 to 1988
>   Oxford Colleges in 1974
>   Yale College in 1969
>   Harvard College in the 1970's (merger with Radcliffe)

The French opened their most elite university somewhat earlier than the U.S. or U.K. Although Leon Blum's new School of Administration in 1936 refused admittance to women, its post-war successor ENA, Ecole nationale de l'Administration, was integrated from its opening in 1946.

Organized religion has similarly been dominated by men since the beginning of recorded history, and this can be understood to some extent in its relation to the man as warrior. In the monotheistic religions, the image of the messiah, as described by the Jewish prophet Isaiah and fulfilled by Jesus, according to Christians, is a man from the lineage of the great warrior king, David, who assumes the throne and brings peace. The spread of Christianity as an organized religion came later when it was adopted by the Roman emperor Constantine (280-337), who established Byzantium as the capital of a new Roman Empire, renamed Constantinople after his death. As for the prophet Mohammad, although he was not primarily a warrior, a turning point in his career was the Battle of Badr which he directed and emerged victorious in the year 624.

In recent years, the Protestant churches have been exceptional with many denominations ordaining women as ministers. In at least one denomination, the Univeralist-Unitarian, the number of women ministers now outnumbers men.

Buddhism has also been male-dominated, although it cannot be explained simply in relation to warfare because the Buddha and the early monks were not warriors. At the First Council of Buddhism, held after the death of the Buddha in the 5th Century BC by 500 male monks, the monk Ananda was put on trial with one of the charges being that he had called for the admission of women into the order. I find no mention of women in later Councils, although the question has been revived in Buddhist circles in recent years. The spread of Buddhism took place during the reign of the renowned warrior and emperor Ashoka who ruled the Mauryan Empire in South Asia from 269 to 232 BC. Ashoka unified a vast empire, at first through warfare and later through wise administration after he came under the influence of the teachings of Buddha and renounced violence throughout his kingdom.

Male domination in the family and economic enterprises, eventually including the rise of great capitalist enterprises, has historically mirrored the male domination of the military, the state, elite education and religion. At the dawn of history, women were subservient to men in the family and barred from most civil participation or the ownership of property in China, Greece and Rome. This was in keeping with religious law as well, as indicated by the Bible for the monotheistic religions and Confucianism in the case of China. Ancient Egypt was exceptional in allowing legal equality to women.

In Europe and its colonies, the legal status of women did not change very much from its Roman precedents until the last few centuries. Up until 1882, when Parliament adopted the Married Women's Property Act, a woman's property in England was considered to be the property of her husband: In France, it was not possible until 1965 for a married woman to work, to open a bank account or to dispose of her own property without the consent of her husband.

Since women could not work or own property they were not able to participate directly in the great development of the capitalist enterprise in the 19th and early 20th Centuries. It is only recently, with legal reforms and access to elite education that women have begun to break through the "glass ceiling" of male domination in the economy.

Violence against women is pervasive in all societies, and much, although not all, can be attributed to the culture of war. The UN Secretary General's Report on Violence against Women (2006) distinguishes the following kinds of violence against women:

1. Violence against women within the family
   (a) Intimate partner violence
   (b) Harmful traditional practices
2. Violence against women in the community
   (a) Femicide: the gender-based murder of a woman
   (b) Sexual violence by non-partners
   (c) Sexual harassment and violence in the workplace, educational institutions and in sport
   (d) Trafficking in women
3. Violence against women perpetrated or condoned by the State
   (a) Custodial violence against women
   (b) Forced sterilization
4. Violence against women in armed conflict

Although violence against women in armed conflict is the last point on the list, an argument can be made that rape and other violence against women has been fundamental to the culture of war over the course of history. This is still true today, although, as the UN report states, it is difficult to document :

> "Although rape in war has been widespread for centuries, it has only recently been recognized as a significant human rights issue. Providing reliable data on the extent of sexual violence in war and humanitarian crises is particularly challenging precisely because of the chaotic circumstances and constantly shifting populations as well as safety considerations. Moreover, many women are reluctant to disclose

> rape, even in order to access support or obtain justice, either for fear of additional reprisals or because of the stigma associated with sexual violence."

When the facts are told about rape in war, they are overwhelming. Here is an excerpt from *Rape: Weapon of Terror* by Sharon Frederick and the AWARE Committee on Rape (2001):

> "World War II documents, the best recorded evidence of wartime rape, reveal assaults numbering at least several hundred thousand, perhaps as many as two million. Thousands in the villages of Russia and Poland, as the Germans invaded early in the war; thousands more when the Soviets got the upper hand and took revenge on the bodies of German women. In the final two weeks of the war, an estimated 100,000 German women were raped in Berlin, by victorious Russian and other Allied troops. In Asia, figures are more exact: at least 20,000 in the Chinese wartime capital of Nanking when the Japanese invaded China; at least 80,000 - perhaps over 100,000 - Korean, Indonesian, Filipino and Chinese women repeatedly raped during their months as sex slaves of the Japanese soldiers."

> "In the decades that followed World War II, the international community paid little attention to, and therefore did little to document, rape during armed conflict though we know a significant number of assaults occurred in areas such as the Congo, Peru, El Salvador, Cambodia and Vietnam ... When Bengal (officially East

Pakistan) declared itself the independent state of Bangladesh, West Pakistani troops quickly moved in to quell the rebellion, and to terrorize the population of 75 million by carrying out widespread rape and murder..."

"During the last decade, rape as a weapon of terror has been documented by news media and international aid organizations in countries including Afghanistan, Kuwait, Algeria, Indonesia, Somalia, Haiti, Kashmir, and Sierra Leone. In the most notorious incidents, more than 20,000 women and girls were raped between 1992 and 1994 as part of the so-called 'ethnic cleansing' in the Balkans. An estimated 200,000 to 400,000 women were raped in Rwanda during the genocidal 1994 war that killed between 500,000 and one million people."

In her ground-breaking book about rape, *Against Our Will,* Susan Brownmiller (1975) argued that rape is an inevitable result of the violence and male domination of the culture of war:

"It has been argued that when killing is viewed as not only permissible but heroic behavior sanctioned by one's government or cause, the distinction between taking a human life and other forms of impermissible violence gets lost, and rape becomes an unfortunate but inevitable by-product of the necessary game called war..."

"War provides men with the perfect psychologic backdrop to give vent to their contempt for women. The very maleness of the military - the brute power of weaponry exclusive to their hands, the spiritual bonding of men at arms, the manly discipline of orders given and orders obeyed, the simple logic of the hierarchical command - confirms what they long suspect, the women are peripheral, irrelevant to the world that counts, passive spectators to the action in the center ring."

Ironically, the criminal justice system with its "eye for an eye" principle, with its disregard for the victim and exclusive concern with punishing the perpetrator, often aggravates the effects of rape by putting the victim through intensive scrutiny and sometimes even accusing her of having caused the rape.

Over the course of history, violence in the family has closely paralleled the subservient status of women, and the culture of war. The most obvious effect is that of wife-beating. There is also a direct relation between the culture of war and family violence against children as shown by cross-cultural analysis. In their paper, *Explaining Corporal Punishment: A Cross-Cultural Study,* Carol and Mel Ember (2005) found a significant relationship of war frequency to violence against the child:

> "In previous research on warfare (Ember and Ember 1992a), we found it important to exclude pacified societies because their warfare frequency was artificially reduced by a colonial power. So we reexamined the relationship between corporal punishment of children and war frequency in nonpacified societies. We found the war frequency is significantly related to corporate punishment in nonpacified societies."

In recent centuries, the culture of war through colonialism and authoritarian rule has adversely affected the family in other ways that have been indirect, but no less destructive. For example, the study mentioned above by Carol and Mel Ember on determinants of corporal punishment of children found that: "corporal punishment of children is likely in societies that are marked by power inequality caused by the presence of social stratification or high levels of political integration, or an alien power (as indicated by a longtime use of alien currency)."

The capitalist exploitation of women and children since the beginning of the industrial revolution, which has been closely linked to the culture of war, has also had a destructive impact on the family. And in more recent years, millions of families have been further decimated by the drug trade and the great rise in prison populations, especially in the United States. As the family has been weakened or destroyed, it is the children, the elderly and the handicapped who suffer the most, since historically their main support came from their role and their sustenance within the context of the extended family. Although the most dramatic and oppressive effects have been on the families of the poor, the families of the middle classes have not escaped. The modern globalized economy demands frequent household moves, long hours and multiple employments and increased frequency of both parents working. Once again, it is the children, the elderly and the handicapped who suffer most.

12. Religion and the culture of war

Throughout history, warfare has been carried out in the name of religion, for example during the crusades of the Middle Ages, and most recently in the justifications given for warfare by Al Qaeda (Islam) and George Bush

(Christianity) with the war policies of Israel (Judaism) as a major issue of contention.

At the beginning of history, religion was an integral aspect of the culture of war. As summarized by Leslie A. White (1959) in *The Evolution of Culture,* all warring cultures enlisted religious institutions in their cause:

> "It may safely be said that no war can be fought without recourse to the supernatural. In civil society it is the business of the clergy, as it was of the medicine man in tribal cultures, to mobilize the population for military purposes. The principal god of the Aztecs was Uitzilopochtli, the god of war, and his priest was one of the two heads of the ecclesiastical hierarchy. Military expeditions were led by priests and the idols of gods. And one of the chief functions of war among the Aztecs was to obtain captives for the temple sacrifices. In Egypt and other ancient cultures of the Old World, victory in war was a gift of the gods: 'Amon has given to me his victory,' declared Rameses II after the battle of Kadesh. And consequently, the gods must be rewarded by gifts to, or a division of the spoils of war with, the priesthoods."

Religious institutions have traditionally played an important role in supporting the internal culture of war by masking its force with elaborate rituals and teachings. As described by White (1959) in an earlier quotation from *The Evolution of Culture,* they have used theology and ritual to install obedience, docility and loyalty to the established order.

The relationship between war and religious institutions was so close at the dawn of civilization that White speaks not of the "state" but of the "state-church" as the ruling institution of society, and he provides numerous examples to make the point (see the earlier section on *religion and the origin of the state*).

On the other hand, most of today's major religions are based on the teachings of prophets who called for non-violence. As mentioned earlier, the teaching of non-violence goes back to a period in early history which has been called by one major philosopher, the Axial Age, at which time most of today's major religions originated.

As a general rule, when religion and state are linked, the religion tends to justify the state's culture of war. With a few exceptions such as the one mentioned earlier (King Ashoka of ancient India) the opposite tends not to be true, that the state adopts the religion's belief in non-violence. Addressing this problem, a major issue in recent centuries has been the demand for separation of church and state. But this is not always achieved, and in some cases there are state religions which are used to justify a culture of war. Examples today include the state of Iran (Islam) and the state of Israel (Judaism). In the United States with its strident militarism, President George W. Bush made frequent reference to his Christian faith (he claims to be a "born-again" Christian) and there is a strong political influence of the so-called "Religious Right".

The relation of religion to the culture of war has always been complex, with a struggle inside each religion between the support of state violence, on the one hand, and insistence on non-violence, on the other hand. An overview is provided by Elise Boulding (2000), in her book *Cultures of Peace: The Hidden Side of History*:

"Every religion then contains two cultures: the culture of violence and war and the culture of peaceableness. The holy war culture calls for mobilization against evil and is easily politicized. The culture of the peaceable garden relies on a sense of the oneness of humankind, often taking the form of intentional communities based on peaceful and cooperative lifeways, sanctuaries for the nonviolent...."

"The Holy War Culture

The holy war culture is a male warrior culture headed by a patriarchal warrior-god. It demands the subjection of women and other aliens to men, the proto-patriarchs, and to God (or the gods). We see it in the ancient Babylonian epics, in the Iliad, in the Bhagavad Gita, in the Hebrew scriptures used by Jews and Christians, and in the Koran..."

"The Peaceable Garden Culture...

Judaism. Practical utopian-pacifist activism is well-exemplified in that form of Zionism represented by Martin Buber. He saw a Jewish national community in Palestine as a opportunity to create a model political community embodying the highest spiritual values of Judaism while practicing a nonviolent reconciling relationship with Arab brothers and sisters as co-tillers of the same soil..."

"Islam. Sufism is the best-known pacifist tradition in Islam, and while the special service of the Sufi is to be a silent witness to God, the Sufi play a special role within the polity, standing over against bureaucracy and formalism..."

"Christianity. Mystical and contemplative traditions in Christianity, as in Islam, are themselves a source of peace witness, with monks and nuns considered role models for peace in the larger community and prayer interpreted as a form of social action. Turning to the Christian activist tradition, we find the Anabaptists and a strong social action wing of Catholicism... Their later descendents include Quakers, Mennonites, and Brethren, now known as the historic peace churches."

13. The arts and the culture of war

The mass media has replaced the arts as the principal propaganda tool of the culture of war. It is no longer so necessary for the emperor to employ artists in the construction and decoration of monuments and murals and coins that glorify military victory and military conquerors, because CNN and Fox News, like the "yellow press" of an earlier generation, can reach a much larger audience and more quickly.

In extreme cases, the arts are still mobilized by the state to justify war. For example the propaganda films of Leni Rieffenstahl supported the policies of the German Nazi government. Similarly, the films produced during the war in the allied countries of Russia, England and the U.S. also served as propaganda for the war effort. On the other hand, when countries are not at war, in recent centuries, the arts have remained more independent of the state and often they are neutral or convey messages against war and the culture of war.

I will not try to make a global survey of this question, but assume that a few observations about the experience we have in the last few decades in the United States probably does not differ greatly from what has happened elsewhere.

At times, the government censors films and other artistic creations that call into question the culture of war. During the McCarthy era of the Cold War in the United States, Congressman Richard Nixon, later to be President, led government hearings to investigate so-called "communist" influences in Hollywood, and, as a result ten major film directors were "blacklisted" so that they could no longer make films. They became known as the "Hollywood Ten."

Aside from the matter of government control, an effective analysis of the arts needs to be done from a class perspective: arts for the ruling class; and arts for the ordinary people. With a few exceptions such as popular music to be discussed below, most artists can only make money by directing their creations to the tastes of the ruling class, and this class, under the present structure of society, is strongly linked, consciously or unconsciously, to the culture of war. Under these circumstances, rather than provide images or creations to justify this culture, many artists get around the question by avoiding political issues altogether.

An important exception, at least in recent years, has been the politicization of popular music. Anti-war music has proliferated during times of disputed wars such as the War in Vietnam and the present war in Iraq. Odetta, Bob Dylan and John Lennon were heroes to the anti-war movement of the 60's and more recently, the Dixie Chicks gained notoriety over their criticism of the War in Iraq. As a result, Lennon was the object of investigations and harassment by the government, and for a time, the songs of the Dixie Chicks were banned from the radio by most of the major media networks.

Thanks to technological advances in the reproduction of music that has made it so widely available, government and media censorship often increases the popularity of music, thus having the opposite effect from that intended by the censors. In the U.S. this was the case for the songs of Lennon and of the Dixie Chicks which gained more popularity than ever as a result of the attacks on them. Censorship had a similar effect in the Soviet Union. I recall my first chance meeting with a young lad when we were waiting in line at a cinema in Moscow in 1976. When he saw that I was an American, he confided in me that he loved the Beatles' music, but that he was in a dilemma because it was banned by the authorities. Should he or should he not buy a contraband tape of the Beatles which was being spread rapidly through the adolescent underground thanks to the availability of tape recorders? Whatever the final decision of this lad, there is no question that many young people did circulate contraband music, and this kind of dilemma, cleverly encouraged by the West, played a role in the loss of legitimacy of the Soviet political system.

14. Nationalism

Nationalism is a relatively recent phenomenon, and it has become an essential element of the culture of war promoted by the state. This is described simply in the following excerpt from the paper *Religious Nationalism and Human Rights* by Little (1994):

> "The notions of 'nation' and 'nationalism,' as we use them today, are relatively recent, and so is the passion for achieving 'national self-determination.' Up through the Middle Ages, it was not customary in Europe to draw sharp political boundaries between different 'peoples,' each of whom shared a distinctive language and culture. In fact, our 'modern world' came into being as one people strove to define themselves over against others by securing and centralizing the means of government and armed defense on their own behalf. So occurred the modern preoccupation with building the 'nation-state.' A people or nation did not achieve self-fulfillment until it ran its own state."

> "... Above all, a nation is supposed to be something one will die for, if need be. It is certainly something that inspires self-denial on behalf of the greater group. ('Ask not what your country can do for you. Ask only what you can do for your country.')"

In recent history, when a state prepares to go to war against another state, or when a people prepares to go to war to seek its freedom against an occupying power (i.e. wars of national liberation), appeals are usually made to nationalism and patriotism and people are urged to prepare for sacrifice, even death, on behalf of their nation. Often nationalism is associated with a state religion or a state language to the extent that legitimacy is denied to other religions or languages. The extreme case was that of Nazi Germany where the claim was made that there was a national race and that it was genetically superior to other races. In such extreme cases of nationalism, other nations are seen to be alien or enemy, and nationalism is thus used to justify making war against them.

The argument can be made that some forms of nationalism are not linked to the culture of war, but only serve to promote a sense of identity and an attitude of solidarity among people who share a common history or language.

15. Racism

Hand in hand with the development of African slavery and colonialism came the development of racism, which was used to justify them. We have already seen this in the account quoted earlier from Franz Fanon. Another particularly vivid description is that of Malcolm X (1964) in his *Autobiography*:

> "Book after book showed me how the white man had brought upon the world's black, brown, red, and yellow peoples every variety of the sufferings of exploitation. I saw how since the sixteenth century, the so-called 'Christian trader' white man began to ply the seas in his lust for Asian and African empires, and plunder, and power..."
>
> "...First, always 'religiously,' he branded 'heathen' and 'pagan' labels upon ancient non-white cultures and civilizations. The stage thus set, he then turned upon his non-white victims his weapons of war.
>
> I read how, entering India - half a *billion* deeply religious brown people - the British white man, by 1759, through promises,

trickery and manipulations, controlled much of India through Great Britain's East India Company ... In 1857, some of the desperate people of India finally mutinied - and, excepting the African slave trade, nowhere has history recorded any more unnecessary bestial and ruthless human carnage than the British suppression of the non-white Indian people.

Over 115 million African blacks - close to the 1930's population of the United States - were murdered or enslaved during the slave trade. And I read how when the slave market was glutted, the cannibalistic white powers of Europe then carved up, as their colonies, the richest areas of the black continent..."

"I read... how the white man raped China at a time when China was trusting and helpless. Those original white 'Christian traders' sent into China millions of pounds of opium. By 1839, so many of the Chinese were addicts that China's desperate government destroyed twenty thousand chests of opium. The first Opium War was promptly declared by the white man. Imagine! Declaring *war* upon someone who objects to being narcotized. The Chinese were severely beaten, with Chinese-invented gunpowder.

The Treaty of Nanking made China pay the British white man for the destroyed opium; forced open China's major ports to British trade; forced China to abandon Hong Kong; fixed China's import tariffs so low that cheap

British articles soon flooded in, maiming China's industrial development."

Racism did not disappear with the abolition of slavery and the liberation of European colonies. It has remained an important feature of capitalist exploitation, by which non-white workers are paid lower wages than white workers, splitting labor solidarity and providing higher profits from exploitation. The most extreme example was that of South African Apartheid, but less extreme racism characterizes capitalist countries around the world. According to economist Victor Perlo (1996), the profits gained directly in the United States from the wage differential between white workers and workers of color grew from $56 billion in 1947 to $197 billion in 1992 (figures corrected for inflation). Perlo estimates that the profits gained indirectly by keeping down the wages of white workers, were even greater.

Racism is used to justify internal interventions that would not otherwise be carried out against those belonging to the dominant racial groups of the state. Perhaps the most extreme example of this were the forced labor camps and extermination camps of the Nazis that were justified by the official racism of the regime. But similar racist justifications are used for internal interventions by most of the "civilized" countries. For example, racist assumptions were involved in the internal interventions in the United States against African-American slaves, the genocide of Native Americans, the confinement of Japanese-Americans in concentration camps during World War II, the suppression of urban revolts in predominantly African-American neighborhoods, and, most recently, the arrests and detentions of Hispanic immigrants. It is unlikely that any of these interventions would have been undertaken against white, Anglo-Saxon Americans.

Racism is used by the state and its media to justify its enemy images and its wars and preparations for war. During World War II, the enemy Japanese and Germans were called "gooks" and "krauts" and portrayed as sub-human. At the present time, Arabs and South Asians are the victims of racist portrayals in the Western media and educational systems.

Racism is similarly used by the state and its media and by political demagogues to portray immigrants from the South, whether Arab and African in Europe or Central and South Americans in the U.S., as inferior and potential enemies, blaming them for the unemployment and declining social services created by the policies of capitalist enterprises and the state.

The racism of internal interventions is supported by the teaching of racism by the mass media and educational systems, including the most elite educational systems, and by churches and other religious organizations. For example, growing up in the American South, I was taught by my Sunday School Superintendent at Church School that it was written in the Bible that the "niggers were born to be slaves." Later, teaching in an elite American university, I found that my colleague in the psychology department was teaching a course to claim that the intelligence of African-Americans is genetically lower than the intelligence of those descended from European immigrants. In fact, it was the psychology department at the most elite American University, Harvard, that was most renowned for its claims of genetic inferiority of African-Americans.

SUMMARY OF THE HISTORY OF THE CULTURE OF WAR

In summary, the culture of war has been an integral part of human culture from early in human evolution. Every aspect of human culture has been profoundly influenced by it, including family structure, the upbringing and education of children, distinctions between men and women, the invention and maintenance of the state, the invention and maintenance of exploitation and racism, and the resultant economic systems including international trade and globalization.

By the end of prehistory, the culture of war was probably pervasive, judging by archaeological evidence. The best hypothesis is that ritual warfare was maintained by most societies and, in the long run, this prepared them to survive otherwise catastrophic famines by raiding the supplies of other communities, or defending their own supplies at such a time. The culture of war included both psychological preparation for war through myths, rituals and traditions and physical preparation through the regular practice of combat, ranging from sporting competitions and initiation rites to ritual warfare and periodic raids and feuds. Judging by the cross-cultural analysis of existing ethnographic data, prehistoric culture of war probably included warriors and weapons, authoritarian rule associated with military leadership, control of information through secrecy, identification of an "enemy", education of young men to be warriors, and male domination.

Male domination was pervasive by the end of prehistory because of the need to exclude women from anything concerning warfare and its related activities of big game hunting and metal-working. Women had to be excluded from warfare in order to resolve the contradiction resulting from the fact that war was carried out against the same neighboring groups with which one inter-married. This made it likely that wars would be fought between the husband of a woman on one side and her father and brothers on the other side. Women could not be trusted with the secrets of warfare, and this was essential because raids, which had to be planned in advance, carried the risk of being ambushed and defeated if women revealed the plans to the "enemy".

With the invention of the state, war was transformed. This is true whether or not one accepts the well-known hypothesis that the state evolved out of warfare. Since writing was invented at more or less the same time as the state, we know a great deal about this period from ancient manuscripts.

Warfare took on new functions, two external and one internal. The tribe or group was no longer the principal actor, but instead it was the state that monopolized the means of violence within its borders. The new functions of warfare were in support of the state: external conquest and defense and internal control. Externally, war was used to increase the power and wealth of the state through military victories, plunder and slaves, and it was used to defeat attempts at invasion by other states. Internally, it was used to prevent and/or defeat attempts at insurrection by slaves or other exploited peoples or rival political forces.

Under the state, the culture of war was also transformed in order to serve the new functions of warfare. Power was based on military leadership and a class-structured society that exploited slaves that were taken prisoner through warfare. As a result, the culture of war became more complex, retaining the characteristics inherited from prehistory, as described above, and adding new characteristics, including wealth based on plunder and slavery, an economy based on exploitation (slaves, serfs, etc.), means to deter slave revolts and political dissidents including internal use of military power, prisons and executions, religious institutions that support the government and military, and artistic and literary glorification of military conquest.

From the beginning of recorded history until the present time the culture of war has become more and more monopolized by the state, retaining the three functions: conquest, defense and internal control. Internal war has been and continues to be a taboo topic. The involvement of the state with the culture of war has become stronger over the course of history as the state has prevented the development of warfare by other social structures.

Over the course of time the economic benefits of plunder and slavery have been extended and/or replaced by colonialism and neo-colonialism externally and by feudalism and then capitalist exploitation internally. In reaction to these developments, a fourth function of war has appeared: revolution and national liberation. Revolutionary movements have traditionally been organized along the lines of the culture of war, and, as a result, the states that have emerged as the result of armed revolution have themselves become new cultures of war.

In recent history, the culture of war at the level of the state has been further reinforced by the development of the military-industrial-complex in which a major section of the newly developed capitalist class has joined its forces with the state. Simultaneously, although in secret, the culture of war has come to include the trade of drugs and guns. Internal military intervention has been put at the service of the capitalist class for the suppression of the labor movement and revolts by the unemployed. Racism and nationalism have been added as essential components that justify and support all other aspects of the culture of war.

The greatest change in the culture of war has been the enormous expansion of control of information including control of the mass media, overtly or covertly, by state power and its allies in the military-industrial complex. Other than these changes, however, the fundamental nature of the culture of war has remained remarkably stable; it has become increasingly a monopoly of the state, essential to the maintenance of state power.

The internal functions of the culture of war explain why state power cannot allow a culture of peace. Perhaps the nation-states would be able to devise a new international system through the United Nations that would protect them from external invasion and conquest, but there is no indication that they are willing to abandon their "right" to use force internally, nor are they even willing to discuss the topic which remains, for the most part, a taboo, i.e. forbidden discussion. Under normal conditions, the authoritarian control exerted through the electoral process of so-called democratic governance at the national level, and the control of information through the mass media, religious instruction and educational systems ensure the power of the state.

Of course, there are great differences between states at any given moment in the extent to which their culture of war is evident. The rich states of the North, for example Scandinavia, are in a better position to hide their internal culture of war through provisions of the welfare state and more liberal systems of electoral participation and education while the poorer states of the South are often less able to accomplish this. But this difference itself is a function of the culture of war, as it rests upon the neo-colonial exploitation whereby the Global North continues to get richer at the expense of the Global South. The United Nations system helps to maintain this exploitation through the policies of the UN Security Council which maintains nuclear and political superiority and the World Bank, International Monetary Fund and World Trade Organization which maintain the economic superiority of the North.

In a word, the usefulness of the culture of war at the present time continues to be its support of the unity and power of the state.

Is there an alternative: can a culture of peace be developed to replace the culture of war? I think so, and in that belief I have written two companion books to this book, one a strategy proposal (Adams 2009a) and the other a utopian novella (Adams 2009b).

REFERENCES

Adams, D. (1979) Brain Mechanisms for Offense, Defense and Submission, *Behavioral and Brain Sciences*, 2: 201-241. Available on the Internet at http://www.culture-of-peace.info/bbs/title-page.html

Adams, D. (1983). Why There Are So Few Women Warriors. *Behavior Science Research*. 18 (3): 196-212. Available on the Internet at http://www.culture-of-peace.info/women/title-page.html

Adams, D. (1986). The Role of Anger in the Consciousness Development of Peace Activists: Where Physiology and History Intersect, *International Journal of Psychophysiology*, 4: 157-164. Available on the Internet at http://www.culture-of-peace.info/psychophysiology/title-page.html

Adams, D. (1989). The Seville Statement on Violence: A Progress Report. *Journal of Peace Research* 26 (2): 113-121. Available on the Internet at http://www.culture-of-peace.info/ssov/title-page.html

Adams D. (1991). *The Seville Statement on Violence: Preparing the Ground for the Constructing of Peace.* UNESCO. Available on Internet at http://www.culture-of-peace.info/brochure/titlepage.html

Adams, D. (1992). Biology does not make men more aggressive than women. In *Of Mice and Women: Aspects of Female Aggression*, edited by K. Bjorkvist and P. Niemela, Academic Press, Inc., Pages 17-25. Available on the Internet at http://www.culture-of-peace.info/biology/title-page.html

Adams, D. (1995). Internal Military Interventions in the United States. *Journal of Peace Research*, 32 (2): 197-211. Available on the Internet at http://www.culture-of-peace.info/intervention/title-page.html

Adams, D. (2003). *Early History of the Culture of Peace: A Personal Memoire.* Available only on the Internet at http://www.culture-of-peace.info/history/introduction.html

Adams, D. (2006). Brain mechanisms of aggressive behavior: An updated review. *Neuroscience and Biobehavioral Reviews* 30: 304–318. Available at: http://www.culture-of-peace.info/update/abstract.html

Adams, D. (2007). *Letter to My Academic Friends*, available only on Internet at http://www.culture-of-peace.info/letter/Letter_to_Academic_Friends.pdf

Adams, D. (2009a) *World Peace through the Town Hall: A Strategy for the Global Movement for a Culture of Peace,* Available for reading on-line or for mail-order at http://culture-of-peace.info/books/worldpeace.html

Adams, D (2009b) *I Have Seen the Promised Land: A Utopian Novella.* Available for reading or for mail-order at http://culture-of-peace.info/books/promisedland.html

Aptheker, H. (1943). *American Negro Slave Revolts.* International Publishers, New York.

Arkush E. and C. Stanish (2005) Interpreting Conflict in the Ancient Andes: Implications for the Archaeology of Warfare. *Current Anthropology* 46 (1): 3-28.

Arrian (86-146). *Tactica.* In Brian Campbell. (2004). *Greek and Roman Military Writers: Selected readings.* Routledge.

Bachofen,, J. J. (1861). *Mother Right: An Investigation of the Religious and Juridical Character of Matriarchy in the Ancient World.*

Bacon, D. (2000). School Testing: An Education-Industrial Complex Is Emerging Published in the *Oakland Tribune,* Sunday, April 16, 2000 Available at: http://www.commondreams.org/views/041600-109.htm

Bell, G. (1996). *The Basics of Selection.* Chapman & Hall, New York and London.

Bennetts, S. (2002). Review of *Human Rights in the Ancient World* by Richard Bauman, Routledge Classical Monographs, London and New York, 2000. Available at: http://www.austlii.edu.au/au/journals/AJHR/2001/11

Bernstein, C. (1977). The Cia And The Media: How Americas Most Powerful News Media Worked Hand in Glove with the Central Intelligence Agency and Why the Church Committee Covered It Up. *Rolling Stone Magazine.* Available on the Internet at http://carlbernstein.com/magazine_cia_and_media.php

Bible. King James Version.

Bonta, B. D. Website Peaceful Societies. Available on Internet at http://peacefulsocieties.org

Boulding, E. (1976). *The Underside of History - A View of Women through Time.* Westview Press.

Boulding, E. (2000). *Cultures of Peace: The Hidden Side of History*. Syracuse University Press.

Brownmiller, S. (1975). *Against Our Will.* Simon and Schuster.

Budholai, B. Environmental Protection Laws in the British Era. Available on the Internet at : http://www.legalserviceindia.com/articles/brenv.htm

Carneiro, R. L. (Ed.). (1967). *The Evolution of Society: Selections from Herbert Spencer's Principles of Sociology.* University of Chicago Press.

Carneiro, R. L. (1970). A Theory of the Origin of the State. *Science*, New Series, 169 (3947): 733-738.

Carneiro, R. L. (1987). Review of *Development and Decline: The Evolution of Sociopolitical Organization* by Henri J. M. Claessen; Pieter Van De Velde; M. Estellie Smith. *American Ethnologist.* 14 (4): 756-770

Chippindale, C. and Taçon, P. (1998). *The Archaelogy of Rock Art.* Cambridge: Cambridge University Press.

Claessen,, H. J. M., Van De Velde, P. and Smith, M. E. (1985). *Development and Decline: The Evolution of Sociopolitical Organization,* New York: Bergin & Garvey

Claessen, H. J. M. And Skalnik, P. (1978). *The Early State.* Berlin: Walter de Gruyter.

Cooper, J. M. (1980). *The Army and Civil Disorder.* Westport, CT: Greenwood.

Curtis, J., Tallis, N. and André-Salvini, B. (2005) *Forgotten Empire: The World of Ancient Persia*, University of California Press, 2005

Daniel, J. (2002). Higher Education for Sale, editorial in *Education Today*, publication of the Education Sector of UNESCO. Available with critical commentaries at: http://www.swaraj.org/shikshantar/mceducationforall.htm

Davis-Kimball, J. (1997). Warrior Women of Eurasia. *Archaeology Magazine*, Volume 50 Number 1, January/February.

Deflem, M. (1999). Warfare, Political Leadership, and State Formation: The case of the Zulu Kingdom, 1808-1879. *Ethnology* 38 (4): 371-391.

Derthick, M. (1965). *The National Guard in Politics.* Cambridge, MA: Harvard University Press.

Divale, W. T. (1974). Migration, External Warfare, and Matrilocal Residence *Behavior Science Research* 9: 75-133.

Divale, W. T. and M. Harris (1976). Population, Warfare, and the Male Supremacist Complex, *American Anthropologist.* 78: 521-538.

Dixon, S. (1985). Polybius on Roman Women and Property. *The American Journal of Philology* 106 (2): 147-170.

Dumas, L. J. (1999). *Lethal Arrogance: Human Fallibility and Dangerous Technologies.* St. Martin's Press, New York.

Ecologist, The (2000). Editorial - Criticism of World Trade Organization, World Bank and International Monetary Fund. Available on the Internet at http://findarticles.com/p/articles/mi_m2465/is_6_30/ai_6565 3637/pg_2

Egyptian Museum in Cairo. (2005). Farid Atiya Press, Cairo.

Eibl-Eibesfeldt, I. (1979). *The Biology of Peace and War.* Thames and Hudson, Great Britain.

Eller, C. (2000). *The Myth of Matriarchal Prehistory: Why an Invented Past Will Not Give Women a Future.* Beacon Press.

Ember, C. R. (1978). Myths About Hunter-Gatherers, *Ethnology* 17: 439-448.

Ember, C. R. and M. Ember (1992). Resource Unpredictability, Mistrust, and War: A Cross-Cultural Study. *Journal of Conflict Resolution* 36: 242-262.

Ember, C. R. and M. Ember (2007). War and the Socialization of Children: Comparing Two Evolutionary Models. *Cross-Cultural Research* 41: 96-122.

Ember, M. and C. R. Ember (1971). The Conditions Favoring Matrilocal versus Patrilocal Residence, *American Anthropologist* 73: 571-594.

Ember, M. and C. R. Ember (2001). Making the World More Peaceful: Policy Implications of Cross-Cultural Research. In *Prevention and control of aggression and the impact on its victims,* Manuela Martinez, ed. New York: Kluwer/Plenum, 331-338.

Ember, M. and C. R. Ember (2005). Explaining Corporal Punishment: A Cross-Cultural Study. *American Anthropologist* 107: 609-619.

Ember, M., C. R. Ember, and B. S. Low (2007). Comparing Explanations of Polygyny. *Cross-Cultural Research* 41: 428-440.

Engels F. (1884). *Origin of the Family, Private Property and the State*. International Publishers, New York, 1942. Available on Internet at http://www.marxists.org/archive/marx/works/1884/origin-family/index.htm

Fanon, F. (1959). *Wretched of the Earth*. Excerpts available on the Internet at http://www.marxists.org/subject/africa/fanon/national-culture.htm

Frederick,, S. and the AWARE Committee on Rape. (2001). *Rape: Weapon of Terror*, Global Publishing, River Edge, NJ. Excerpt available on the Internet at http://www.worldscibooks.com/general/etextbook/g063/g063_intro.pdf

Freire,, P. (1968). *Pedagogy of the Oppressed.* Continuum International Publishing Group. Excerpts available on the Internet at http://www.zonalatina.com/Zldata288.htm

Freud, S. (1930). *Civilization and Its Discontents.*

Fried, M. H. (1967). *The Evolution of Political Society: An Essay in Political Anthropology.* New York: Random House.

Friends Committee on National Legislation (2008). Where do our income tax dollars go? Available on Internet at http://www.fcnl.org/pdfs/taxDay08.pdf

Furiati, C. (1994). *ZR Rifle: The Plot to Kill Kennedy and Castro.* Ocean Press. Australia.

Fu Xuan (217-278). Woman (poem). Available on the Internet at http://en.wikipedia.org/wiki/Fu_Xuan

Guilaine, J. and Zammit, J.. (2001). *Le Sentier de la Guerre: Visages de la Violence Prehistorique.* Editions du Seuil, Paris.

Heider, K. G. (1979). *Grand Valley Dani: Peaceful Warriors.* Holt, Rinehart and Winston, Inc.

Herodotus. (~430 BC). *The Persian Wars.* Translated by George Rawlinson. Published by The Modern Library. Random House, 1942.

Ingelstam, L (2000). Democracy and Globalization: On the need for a politics of resistance to the excesses of system capitalism. Available on the Internet at http://www.nnn.se/archive/globedem.htm

International Centre for Prison Studies, Kings College, London. (2008). *World Prison Brief.* Available at: http://www.kcl.ac.uk/depsta/law/research/icps/downloads/wppl-8th_41.pdf

Jaspers, K. (1953). *The Origin and Goal of History*, translated by Michael Bullock, New Haven, CT: Yale University Press.

Johnson, J.H. (2002). Women's Legal Rights in Ancient Egypt. Available on Internet at http://fathom.lib.uchicago.edu/1/777777190170/

Kairatos Internet Site. The Ancient Cities of Crete. Available on the Internet at http://www.kairatos.com.gr/myweb/ancientcitiesknossos-oios.htm

Kuschel, R. (1989). *Vengeance is their Reply: Blood Feuds and Homicides on Bellona Island.* Dansk psykologisk Forlag.

Landis, F. (1982). CIA Psychological Warfare Operations: Case Studies in Chile, Jamaica, and Nicaragua. *Science for the People Magazine*, January/February 1982.

Lenin V. (1917). *The State and Revolution.* Available on the Internet at http://www.marxists.org/archive/lenin/works/1917/staterev/index.htm

Lenin, V. (1917). *War and Revolution.* Available on the Internet at http://www.marxists.org/archive/lenin/works/1917/may/14.htm

Little, D. (1994). Religious Nationalism and Human Rights, in Gerard F. Powers, Drew Christiansen, SJ, and Robert Hennemeyer *(eds.), Peacemaking: Moral and Policy Challenges for a New World,* Washington, DC: U.S. Catholic Conference, pp. 84-95. Available on the website of the United States Institute of Peace at http://www.usip.org/religionpeace/rehr/relignat.html

Mahon, J. K. (1983). *History of the Militia and the National Guard*. Macmillan, New York.

Malcolm X and A. Haley. (1964). *The Autobiography of Malcolm X*. Grove Press, New York.

Maya, A History of The Mayans (2004). Available on Internet at http://history-world.org/maya.htm

McCoy, A. (1997). Drug Fallout: the CIA's Forty Year Complicity in the Narcotics Trade. *The Progressive*. Excerpts available on the Internet at:
http://www.thirdworldtraveler.com/CIA/CIAdrug_fallout.html

Milner, G. R. (1999). Warfare in prehistoric and early historic eastern North America. *Journal of Archaeological Research* 7 (2) 105-151.

Moyers, B. (2002). Bill Moyers Interviews Chuck Spinney. Available on the Internet at:
http://www.pbs.org/now/transcript/transcript_spinney.html

Moyers, B. (2007). "Buying the War" broadcast on PBS television on April 25, 2007. Available on the Internet at http://www.pbs.org/moyers/journal/btw/transcript1.html

Murdock, G. P. (1937). Comparative data on the division of labor by sex. *Social Forces,* 15: 551-553.

Nafissi, M. (2004). Class, Embeddedness, and the Modernity of Ancient Athens. *Comparative Studies in Society and History* 46 (2) 378-410.

Nkrumah, K. (1965). *Neo-Colonialism, the Last Stage of Imperialism*. Available on the Internet at http://www.marxists.org/subject/africa/nkrumah/neo-colonialism/ch01.htm

Otterbein, K. F. (1968). Internal War: A Cross-Cultural Study. *American Anthropologist* 70: 277-289

Otterbein, K. F. (1973). The Anthropology of War. Chapter 21 in *Handbook of Social and Cultural Anthropology.* Edited by J. J. Honigmann. Rand McNally Co.

Perlo,, Victor (1996). *Economics of Racism II: The Roots of Inequality, USA.* New York: International Publishers.

Riker, W. H., (1957). *The Role of the National Guard in American Democracy*. Washington, DC: Public Affairs Press.

Roksandic, M. (2004). How Violent Was the Mesolithic, or Is There a Common Pattern of Violent Interactions Specific to Sedentary Hunter-Gatherers? In *Violent Interactions in the Mesolithic: Evidence and meaning*, edited by M. Roksandic, pp. 1-7. B.A.R. International Series 1237. Oxford: Archaeopress

Scahill, J, (2007) *Blackwater: The Rise of the World's Most Powerful Mercenary Army*, New York: Nation Books.

Schmidt, C. W. (2004). The Price of Preparing for War. *Environmental Health Perspectives*, 112(17), A1004-5, available on the Internet at http://www.pubmedcentral.nih.gov/articlerender.fcgi?artid=1253681

Schulting, R. J. and M. Wysocki (2002). Cranial Trauma in the British Earlier Neolithic, *Past: The Newsletter of the Prehistoric Society*. 41 Available on the Internet at http://www.ucl.ac.uk/prehistoric/past/past41.html#Cranial

Sipes, R. G. (1973). War, sports, and aggression: An empirical test of two rival theories. *American Anthropologist* 75: 64-86.

Spencer, B. and F. J. Gillen. (1927). *The Arunta: A Study of a Stone Age People*. Macmillan.

Spencer, H. (1976-1896). *Principles of Sociology: Vol 1*. Appleton, London.

Sun Tzu (6th Century BC). *On the art of war*. Translated from the Chinese by Lionel Giles (1910). Available on Internet at http://www.chinapage.com/sunzi-e.html

Thompson. , T. J. (2006). An Ancient Stateless Civilization: Bronze Age India and the State in History, *The Independent Review,* 10 (3): 365-384.

Thucydides. (~400 BC). *The Peloponnesian War*. Translated by John. H. Finley, Jr. and Published by The Modern Library. Random House, 1951.

Tutu, D. (1999). *No Future Without Forgiveness.* New York: Doubleday.

UNESCO (1980). *Many Voices One World. Report by the International Commission for the Study of Communication Problems.* Available on the Internet at http://unesdoc.unesco.org/images/0004/000400/040066eb.pdf

UNESCO (1994). *History of Humanity. Volumes I-VII.* Routledge Publishing.

United Nations (1946). *Charter of the United Nations.* Available on the Internet at http://www.un.org/aboutun/charter/index.html

United Nations (1992). *An Agenda for Peace: Preventive diplomacy, peacemaking and peace-keeping.* Document A/47/277. Available on the Internet at http://www.un.org/Docs/SG/agpeace.html

United Nations (1998). *Consolidated report containing a draft declaration and programme of action on a culture of peace.* Document A/53/370. Available on Internet at http://www.culture-of-peace.info/annexes/resA-53-370/coverpage.html

United Nations Office on Drugs and Crime. (2005). *World Drug Report.* Available on the Internet at http://www.unodc.org/pdf/WDR_2005/volume_1_web.pdf

United Nations Secretary-General Report. (2006). *In-depth study on all forms of violence against women* A/61/122/Add.1. Available on the Internet at http://daccessdds.un.org/doc/UNDOC/GEN/N06/419/74/PDF/N0641974.pdf?OpenElement

United States Department of State (2001). *World Military Expenditures and Arms Transfers 1999-2000.* Available on the Internet at http://www.fas.org/man/docs/wmeat9900/table1.pdf

United States Senate. (1986). Senate Committee Report on Drugs, Law Enforcement and Foreign Policy, chaired by Senator John F. Kerry. Excerpts available on the Internet at http://www.geocities.com/iran_contra_christic_institute/

Versnel, H. S. (1990). *Inconsistencies in Greek and Roman Religion*, Brill.

Weber, M. (1921). Politics as a Vocation. In *From Max Weber: Essays in Sociology*, edited by H. H. Gerth and C. Wright Mills, 77-128. New York: Oxford University Press.

White, L. A. (1959). *The Evolution of Culture.* New York: McGraw-Hill.

Wiener, J. (2005). *Historians in Trouble: Plagiarism, Fraud and Politics in the Ivory Tower*, New York, The New Press.

Wikipedia Free Encyclopedia. Available on Internet at http://en.wikipedia.org/wiki/Main_Page

Wright, Q. (1942). *A Study of War.* University of Chicago Press.

Xenophon (~375 BC). In Brian Campbell. (2004). *Greek and Roman Military Writers: Selected readings.* Routledge.

INDEX

Abolitionist Movement, 135
Abraham, David, 116
Academia, 116
Adams, David, 1, 20, 22, 37, 38, 147, 180, 181, 182
Afghanistan, 95, 128, 129, 132, 135, 162
African Bushmen, 30
Agaev, Ednan, 125
aggression, 17, 186, 192
agriculture, 4, 6, 30, 32, 34, 36, 44, 72, 83, 105, 111, 112, 118
Air America, 127, 128
Al Qaeda, 164
Alexander the Great, 149
Algeria, 31, 107, 137, 162
Allende, Salvador, 94, 133, 137
An Agenda for Peace, 96, 193
André-Salvini, B., 45, 185
anti-personnel mines, 120
Aptheker, H., 110, 182

Aristotle, 60
Arkush, E., 12, 182
armaments, 40, 87, 94, 95, 99, 100, 126
Arrian, 64, 183
artists, 42, 49, 169
arts, 41, 47, 55, 64, 78, 87, 99, 106, 133, 168, 169, 178
Arunta, 34, 192
Ashoka, 70, 158, 166
Ashurbanipal, 45, 47
Australia, 135, 188
Australian aborigines, 33, 36
authoritarian, 3, 16, 40, 42, 56, 67, 87, 99, 133, 136, 138, 150, 164, 176, 179
AWARE Committee on Rape, 161, 187
Axial Age, 86, 166
Aztec, 76, 98
Bachofen, Johann Jakob, 24, 183
Bacon, D., 153, 183
banking concept, 151, 152
Beatles, 170
Bell, G., 13, 183
Bennetts, S., 90, 183

Bernstein, Carl, 145, 183
Bible, 50, 72, 73, 74, 159, 175, 183
blacklists, 169
Blackwater, 115, 191
Blum, Leon, 149, 157
Bonta, B., 3, 183
Boulding, Elise, 24, 86, 166, 183
bourgeois democracy, 122, 134, 135
Brownmiller, Susan, 162, 184
Buber, Martin, 167
Buddha, 86, 158
Buddhist, 70, 158
Budholai, B., 117, 184
Bush, George H., 145
Bush, George W., 37, 139, 142, 150, 164, 166
Caesar, 84, 149
Cambridge, 150, 157, 184, 185
Capital punishment, 122
capitalist, 6, 92, 93, 99, 107, 112, 137, 147, 156, 159, 164, 174, 175, 178

Carneiro, Robert, 27, 79, 80, 81, 83, 184
Castro, Fidel, 95, 128
Catal Huyuk, 25
Central America, 40, 42, 101, 129
Central Intelligence Agency, 127, 183
Chavez, Hugo, 137
Chernobyl, 120
Chile, 94
China, 40, 52, 53, 54, 55, 79, 86, 89, 96, 100, 107, 112, 121, 126, 127, 159, 161, 173
Chippindale, C., 31, 184
Christianity, 158, 165, 166, 168, 172
Christic Institute, 130
church, 20, 83, 84, 166
Church Committee, 145, 183
Church, Frank, 145
CIA, 94, 106, 127, 128, 129, 131, 141, 142, 145, 146, 148, 150, 189, 190
Civil War, 110, 111, 135
Claessen, H.-J. M., 81, 184

class, 2, 3, 7, 19, 44, 50, 54, 55, 60, 76, 79, 80, 85, 88, 90, 91, 93, 112, 117, 121, 137, 150, 164, 169, 177, 178
Clinton, Hilary, 156
cluster bombs, 120
CNN, 168
Cohen, Ronald, 81
Cold War, 95, 100, 114, 120, 124, 129, 147, 148, 169
Colombia, 79, 94, 132
colonialism, 93, 94, 101, 102, 103, 104, 106, 109, 112, 164, 172, 178, 191
Confucianism, 159
Confucius, 56, 86
conquest, 41, 68, 80, 87, 92, 99, 101, 126, 177, 178, 179
Constantine, 158
Contra War, 129, 133, 142
Cooper, J. M., 111, 184
Crete, 41, 66, 67, 68, 69, 83, 86, 189
criminal justice, 121
Cro-Magnon, 31

CRS, 112
crusades, 164
Cuba, 95, 134, 144, 148
cultural evolution, 1, 37
Culture of Peace News Network, 120
Curtis, J., 45, 185
Dahomeans, 98
Dani, 7, 8, 9, 10, 11, 18, 36, 188
Daniel, John, 152, 185
Darius, 66
Dark Ages, 93
Davis-Kimball, J., 31, 185
De Laet, S., 6
Deflem, Mathieu, 81, 185
DeGaulle, Charles, 96
democracy, 17, 60, 91, 109, 133, 134, 135, 136, 138, 140, 141, 144
democratic participation, 136, 137
depleted uranium, 120
Derthick, M., 112, 185
Divale, W. T., 23, 25, 28, 185
Dixie Chicks, 170
Dixon, Suzanne, 62, 185

Djebel Sahaba, 31
Donohue, Phil, 143
Dreyfus, Alfred, 149
drugs, 93, 99, 127, 128, 129, 130, 131, 132, 142, 178
Dumas, Lloyd J., 120, 185
Dylan, Bob, 169
Ecole Militaire, 148, 149
Ecologist, 108, 186
education, 16, 41, 45, 48, 52, 62, 63, 87, 99, 109, 148, 149, 150, 151, 152, 153, 154, 157, 159, 176, 179
Egypt, 40, 41, 49, 50, 51, 52, 72, 79, 83, 89, 98, 157, 159, 165, 189
Eibl-Eibesfeldt, I., 4, 30, 33, 186
Eisenhower, Dwight, 124
Elijah, Isaiah and Jeremiah, 86
Eller, C., 25, 186
Ember, Carol and Mel, 4, 5, 17, 23, 26, 27, 30, 32, 163, 164, 186

enemy, 4, 6, 8, 9, 10, 16, 20, 36, 40, 41, 42, 50, 57, 70, 86, 87, 99, 114, 115, 133, 147, 148, 172, 175, 176, 177
Engels, Friedrich, 90, 109, 116, 187
England, 98, 135, 157, 159, 168
environment, 13, 14, 60, 68, 87, 99, 109, 117, 120, 124
European Union, 113
exploitation, 3, 41, 42, 44, 87, 93, 99, 101, 108, 109, 111, 112, 117, 136, 137, 164, 172, 174, 176, 178, 179
failed state, 97
family, 19, 22, 40, 54, 62, 63, 73, 78, 154, 159, 160, 163, 164, 176, 187
Fanon, Franz, 103, 172, 187
Federal Communication Commission, 139
feudalism, 93, 112, 178
feuding, 6, 11, 26, 33, 35, 36, 132
Finland, 135

first Gulf War, 134
Fox News, 168
France, 31, 96, 100, 112, 135, 149, 150, 159
Frazer, James, 19
Frederick, S., 161, 187
free enterprise, 138
Freire, Paulo, 150, 187
Freud, Sigmund, 37, 187
Fried, M. H., 82, 187
Friends Committee on National Legislation, 100, 188
Fu Xuan, 54, 188
Furiati, C., 128, 188
Ganda, 98, 123
Gandhi, Mahatma, 122
Ghana, 103, 107
Gilgamesh, 43
Gillen, F. J., 34, 192
Gorbachev, Mikhail, 125, 148
Gortyn Laws, 68
Grandes Écoles, 150
Great Britain, 104, 173, 186
Greece, 40, 42, 44, 51, 58, 60, 61, 62, 63, 67, 68, 79, 84, 92, 117, 149, 159, 194
Grenada, 146

Guevara, Che, 95
Guilaine, J., 31, 188
Hamas, 137
Harappan, 41, 71, 72, 82, 83, 86
Harris, M., 28, 185
Harvard, 148, 150, 157, 175, 185
Hatshepsut, 51, 157
Hearst, Randolph, 144
Hebrew, 41, 50, 72, 75, 167
Heider, Karl, 7, 188
Herodotus, 46, 188
Hitler, Adolf, 133
Hollywood, 106, 107, 169
Hollywood Ten, 169
holy war culture, 86, 167
Hull, John, 131
human rights, 123, 133, 160
Huns, 92
hunter-gatherers, 6, 30, 32, 33, 36
hunting, 4, 6, 14, 19, 22, 24, 28, 30, 31, 32, 33, 45, 47, 156, 176
Huntington, Samuel, 148
Iliad, 58, 167
IMF, 108

imperialism, 94, 103, 106, 118
Inca, 98, 123
India, 31, 40, 46, 71, 79, 84, 86, 117, 166, 172, 192
Indus, 41, 69, 71
information, control of, 3, 16, 41, 57, 64, 87, 93, 99, 130, 138, 140, 141, 145, 146, 176, 179
Ingelstam, L., 126, 188
initiation rites, 17, 18, 24, 28, 63, 156, 176
internal military intervention, 1, 3, 88, 92, 94, 99, 109, 110, 111, 113, 114, 115, 116, 149, 165, 178, 179, 182
International Centre for Prison Studies, 188
International Monetary Fund, 105, 108, 109, 180, 186
International Telephone and Telegraph, 94
internet, 138
Iran-Contra Scandal, 129, 130
Iraq, 37, 94, 95, 115, 134, 139, 142, 169
Islam, 164, 166, 167, 168
Israel, 52, 73, 86, 156, 165, 166
Italy, 31, 89, 104, 126, 135
Jainism, 86
Jamaica, 146, 189
Jaspers, Karl, 86, 188
Jericho, 72, 73
Jesus, 86, 90, 158
Johnson, J. H., 51, 189
Johnson, Lyndon, 37
Joshua, 73
Judaism, 165, 166, 167
Kairatos, 69, 189
Kautsky, Karl, 136
Kennedy, John F., 128
Kerry, John F., 130, 194
King David and King Solomon, 73
Korea, 136
Kung bushmen, 30
Kuschel, Rolf, 35, 189
Kuwait, 135, 162
labor, 42, 44, 74, 77, 80, 85, 106, 108, 111, 113, 133, 134, 136, 174, 178
Landis, Fred, 146, 189

Lenin, Vladimir, 102, 136, 189
Lennon, John, 169
Liebling, A.J., 140
Little, D., 170, 189
Livni, Tzipi, 156
Livy, 66
Low, B.S., 27, 187
MacBride report, 139
MacBride, Sean, 139
Mafia, 127, 128, 129
Mahon, J.K., 110, 112, 190
Malcolm X, 172, 190
male domination, 16, 20, 21, 22, 24, 25, 27, 28, 29, 41, 48, 51, 53, 75, 77, 87, 99, 133, 156, 158, 159, 162, 167, 176
Mao Tse-Tung, 56, 149
marriage, 19, 21, 22, 23, 25, 26, 48, 78
Marx, Karl, 90, 109, 116
mass media, 93, 95, 106, 114, 133, 142, 145, 146, 147, 148, 168, 175, 179
matriarchy, 24
matrilocality, 22, 25, 26, 27
Maurya, 66, 70, 158
Mayans, 75, 78, 190
Mazdakian revolt, 89
McCarthy, Joseph, 114, 117, 169
McCoy, Alfred, 128, 190
McDonaldization of education, 152, 153
Mennonites, 168
Mesolithic, 4, 30, 31, 191
Mesopotamia, 40, 42, 44, 45, 46, 47, 48, 49, 52, 79, 84, 98
metal-working, 28, 176
military spending, 100, 126
military-industrial complex, 93, 95, 98, 99, 123, 124, 125, 126, 127, 139, 179
Milner, G. R., 5, 190
Minoan, 66, 67, 68
Mohammad, 86, 158
Mongols, 92
Moos, Malcolm, 125
Moyers, Bill, 124, 142, 144, 190
multi-national corporation, 93, 94, 95
Murdock, George, 28, 190

Nafissi, M., 60, 190
Napoleon, 148, 149
national guard, 90
national liberation, 93, 98, 103, 171, 178
nationalism, 93, 98, 99, 170, 171, 172, 179, 189
NATO, 96, 132
Nazi, 114, 168, 171
Neanderthal, 31
neo-colonialism, 93, 101, 103, 104, 178
Neolithic, 3, 4, 6, 7, 30, 31, 32, 192
New York Times, 129, 145
New Zealand, 135
Nicaragua, 129, 133, 135, 146, 189
Nigeria, 94
Nixon, Richard, 169
Nkrumah, Kwame, 103, 106, 108, 191
non-state societies, 5, 7, 16, 18, 27
non-violence, 70, 86, 166
North, Oliver, 129, 131
nuclear weapons, 37, 100
nuclear winter, 120
Odetta, 169
Opium Wars, 127
Otterbein, K. F., 23, 80, 191
Oxford, 150, 157, 191, 194
Paleolithic, 4, 30, 31
Palestine, 137, 167
paramilitary forces, 95
patrilocal exogamy, 21, 26
patrilocality, 22, 23, 26, 156
peaceful peoples, 4
Pekangekun, 30
Peloponnesian Wars, 58
Perlo, Victor, 174, 191
Peru, 79, 83, 161
pharaohs, 49, 50, 51, 52, 83, 157
Philippines, 133
Pinochet, Augusto, 137
Plan Colombia, 132
police, 90, 91, 94, 110, 112
pollution, 117, 118, 119
Polybius, 62
polygyny, 27
Polynesia, 79
Powell, Colin, 139
prehistory, 3, 4, 7, 14, 16, 21, 22, 25, 30, 31, 48, 86, 176, 177

prisoners of war, 44, 47, 50
prisons, 41, 87, 88, 90, 91, 178
private army, 95
private property, 6, 28, 44, 51, 53, 62, 66, 74, 78, 90, 122, 123, 135, 159, 185, 187
private war, 98
propaganda, 41, 48, 62, 66, 75, 87, 91, 95, 99, 106, 107, 133, 142, 143, 144, 146, 148, 168
Protestantism, 135, 158
psychological warfare, 146, 147
punishment, 38, 39, 40, 90, 111, 116, 122, 123, 163, 164
Qin Dynasty, 55
Quakers, 168
Queen Victoria, 157
racism, 93, 98, 99, 102, 150, 172, 174, 175, 176
Ramsses, 50
rape, 144, 160, 161, 162, 163
Rather, Dan, 143
Reagan, 117, 129, 148
Reagan administration, 117
Red Army, 113
religion, 8, 19, 20, 41, 46, 47, 48, 53, 55, 67, 68, 70, 76, 78, 84, 85, 86, 87, 91, 92, 99, 106, 107, 133, 134, 135, 156, 157, 158, 159, 164, 165, 166, 167, 171, 175, 178, 179
Religious Right, 166
revenge, 11, 98, 161
revolts, 41, 87, 88, 90, 110, 111, 121, 174, 178, 179
revolution, 93, 110, 112, 164, 178
revolutionary, 93, 95, 98, 103, 106, 112, 128, 155
Rice, Condoleezza, 156
Rieffenstahl, Leni, 168
Rigveda, 41, 69, 70
Riker, W. H., 111, 112, 191
ritual warfare, 6, 8, 12, 176
rock-painting, 30
Roksandic, M., 32, 191

Roman, 25, 61, 62, 64, 66, 85, 90, 92, 156, 158, 159, 185, 194
Roman Catholic Church, 85, 156
Rome, 44, 58, 61, 62, 79, 84, 90, 117, 149, 159
Russia, 31, 96, 100, 114, 161, 168
Rwanda, 162
Saudi Arabia, 135
Scahill, Jeremy, 115, 191
Scandinavia, 84, 179
Schmidt, C. W., 118, 191
school texts, 154
Schulting, R. J., 5, 192
second Gulf War, 134
secrecy, 3, 16, 20, 21, 41, 57, 62, 64, 65, 87, 99, 132, 133, 138, 141, 142, 176
Service, Elwood, 82
Seville Statement on Violence, 1, 36
Shang dynasty, 53
Sipes, R. G., 17, 192
Skull and Bones, 150

slavery, 3, 28, 41, 50, 53, 60, 64, 70, 74, 77, 86, 87, 93, 110, 111, 135, 172, 174, 178
slaves, 41, 42, 43, 44, 50, 53, 54, 55, 58, 68, 69, 74, 75, 77, 79, 80, 87, 89, 90, 91, 110, 135, 161, 174, 175, 177
socialism, 106, 116, 133, 137, 138, 146, 149
Socrates, 63, 90
South Africa, 118, 122, 133
Soviet, 95, 113, 114, 120, 125, 128, 133, 148, 170
Soviet Empire, 95, 113
Sparta, 63, 89
Spartacus, 89
Spencer, B., 34, 192
Spencer, Herbert, 27, 80, 83, 184, 192
Spinney, Chuck, 124, 190
sports, 11, 17, 29, 192
Stalin, Joseph, 113, 133
Stanish, C., 12, 182
Sufism, 167
Sumer, 84

Sun Tzu, 56, 57, 65, 192
Sweden, 31, 126
taboo, 18, 91, 92, 113, 114, 116, 117, 120, 127, 129, 140, 178, 179
Taçon, P., 31, 184
Taleban, 95
television, 124, 137, 138, 142, 147, 190
territory, 6, 10, 14, 32, 33, 42, 43, 63, 79, 82, 95, 97, 103, 128
Thompson, T. J., 71, 192
Thucydides, 58, 64, 65, 92, 192
Trotsky, Leon, 113
Truth and Reconciliation Commission, 122
Turks, 92
Tutankhamum, 50
Tutu, Bishop Desmond, 122, 192
Tylor, Edward B., 98
UN Secretary General's Report on Violence against Women, 159
UN Security Council, 95, 180
UNESCO, 6, 41, 42, 46, 47, 48, 49, 50, 52, 53, 54, 55, 61, 62, 66, 67, 68, 69, 70, 71, 75, 76, 77, 78, 87, 88, 92, 139, 140, 148, 152, 181, 185, 192, 193
United Nations, 87, 93, 95, 96, 108, 113, 122, 125, 132, 133, 134, 135, 179, 180, 193
Upanishads, 86
Venezuela, 137
Versnel, H.S., 69, 194
Vietnam, 37, 107, 127, 129, 161, 169
violence against women, 159, 160, 193
Wall Street, 104
weapons, 4, 9, 16, 18, 22, 24, 25, 28, 29, 30, 31, 63, 67, 69, 120, 124, 131, 156, 172, 176
Weber, Max, 82, 97, 194
Western Zhou Dynasty (1027-771 BC, 54
White, Leslie A., 1, 24, 83, 87, 88, 97, 122, 165, 194
Wiener, J., 116, 194

Wikipedia, 66, 97, 194
Wilson, Woodrow, 144
Women's Suffrage, 135
World War II, 125, 135, 147, 149, 161, 174, 175
Wright, Quincy, 33, 115, 194
writing, invention of, 41

Wysocki, M., 5, 192
Xenophon, 63, 194
Xiongnu, 92
Yahgan, 30
Yale, 150, 157, 188
Zammit, J., 31, 188
Zoroastrianism, 86
Zulu Kingdom, 81, 82, 185

Made in the USA
Monee, IL
11 October 2022